THIS COLORING BOOK BELONGS TO:

- - - - - - - - - - - - - - - - -

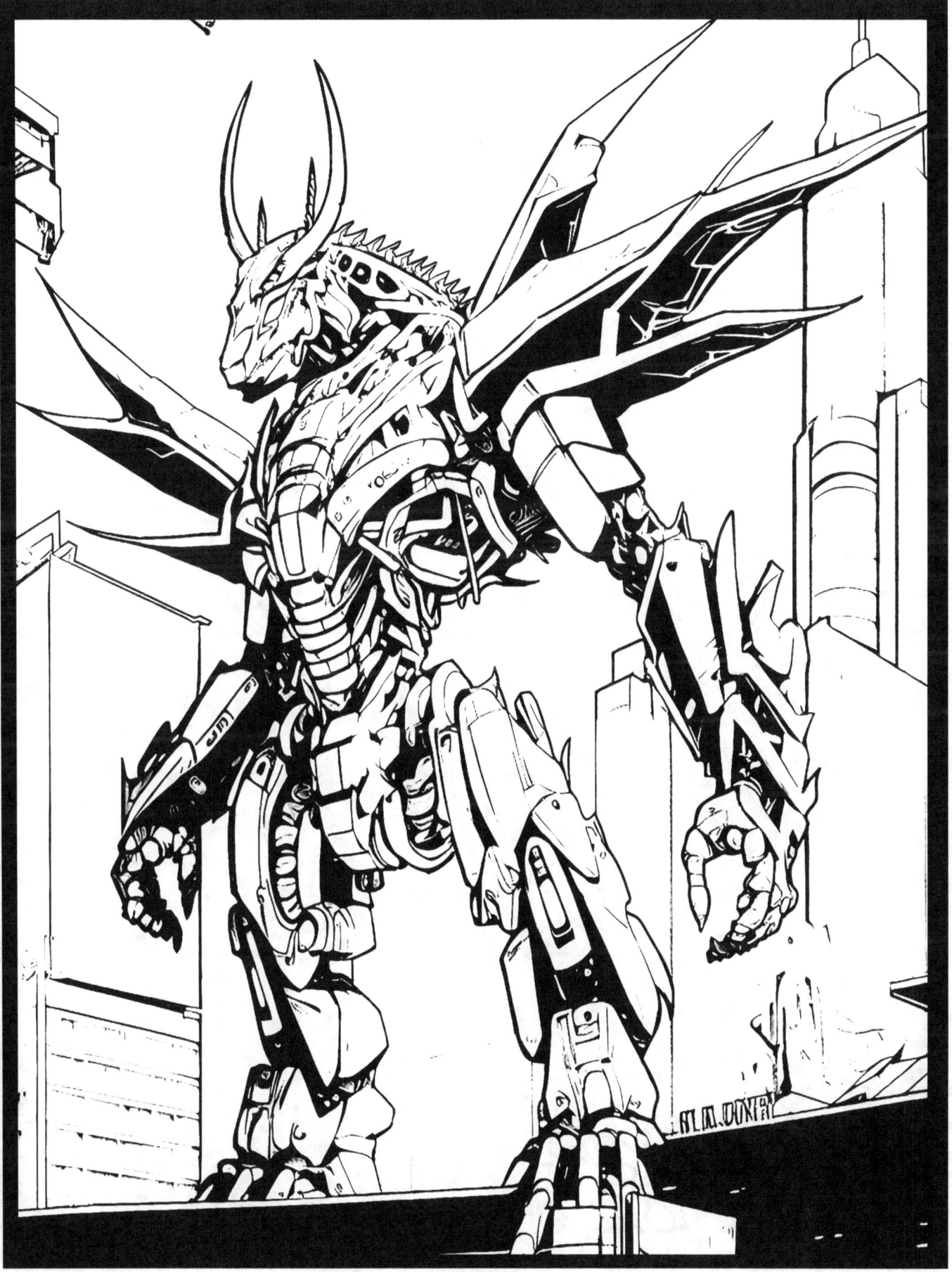

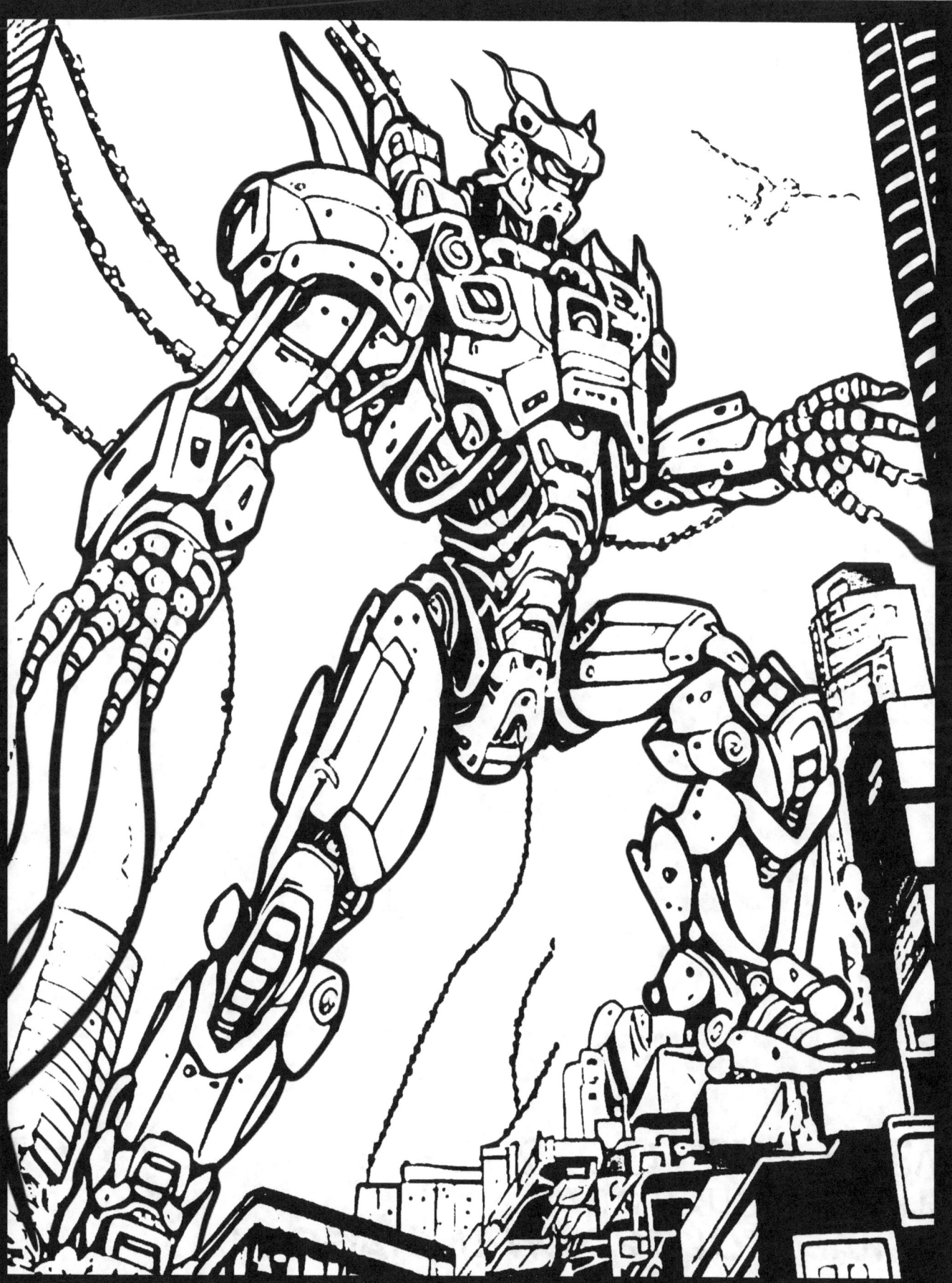

MECH SUIT 002238475
SUBMIT YOUR ART AT:
@IMAGICOLORZ ON INSTAGRAM

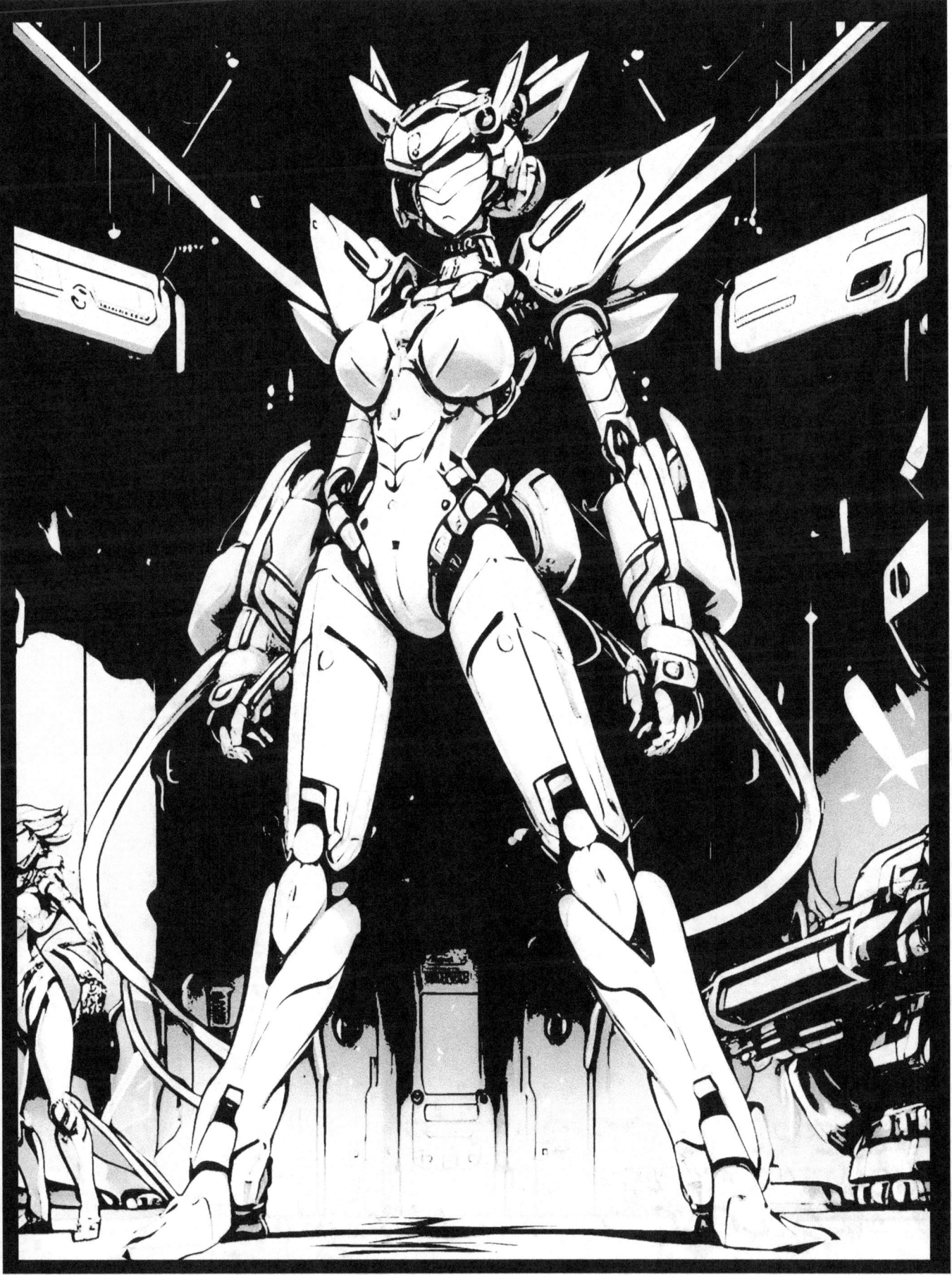

THE GRIME OF BATTLE

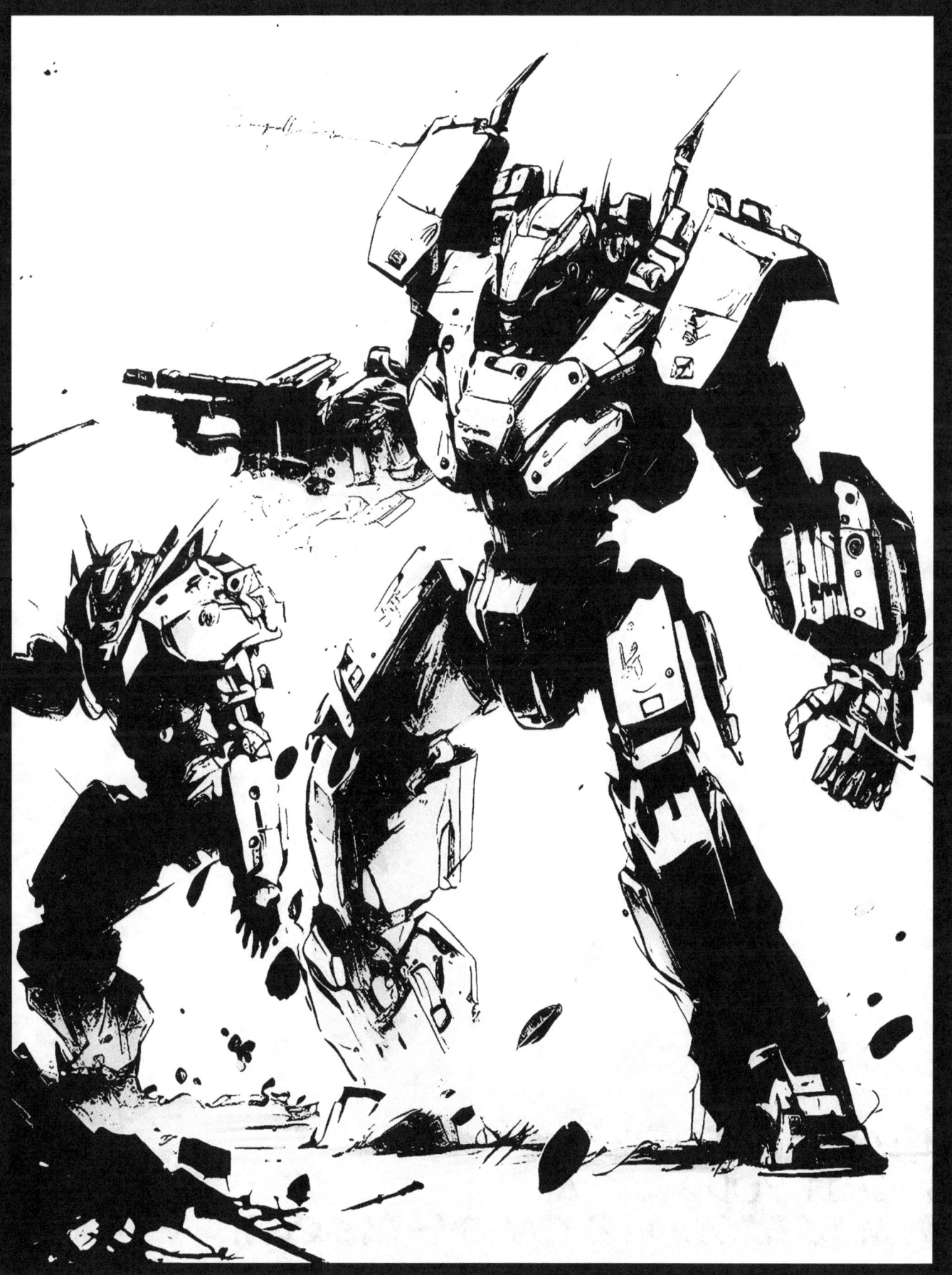

HEAVY PATROL
SUBMIT YOUR ART AT:
@IMAGICOLORZ ON INSTAGRAM

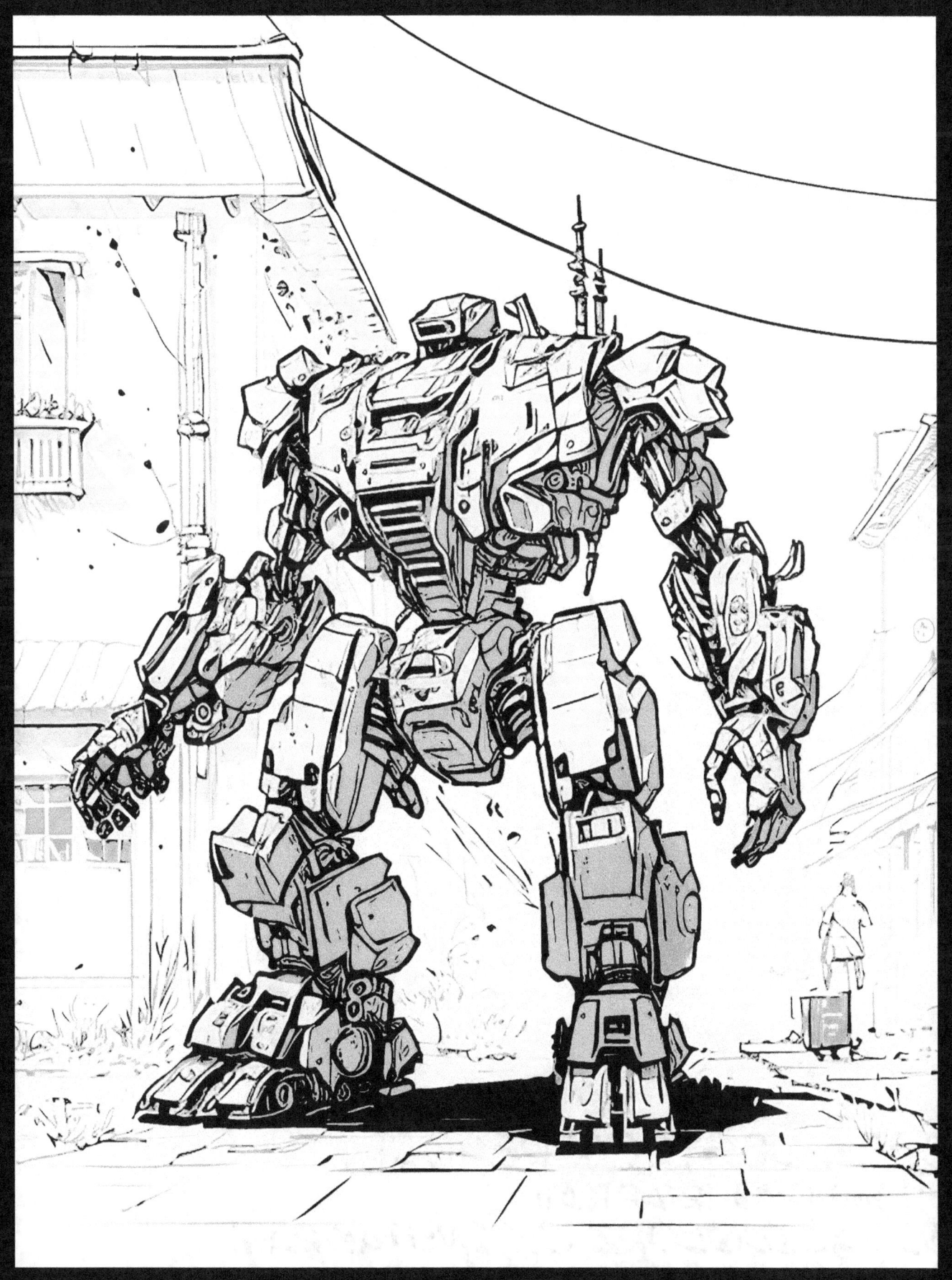

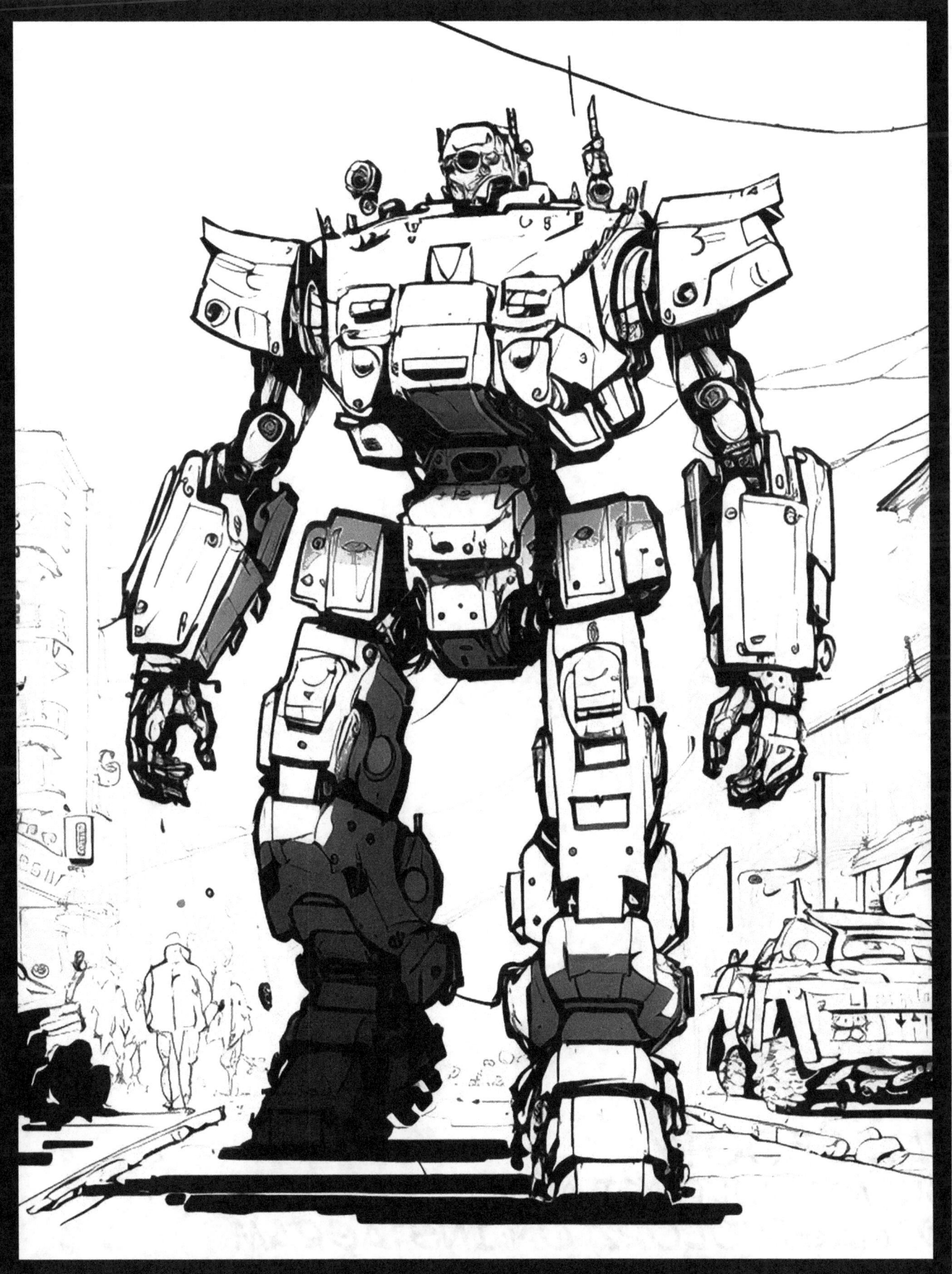

TANK FOOTY
SUBMIT YOUR ART AT:
@IMAGICOLORZ ON INSTAGRAM

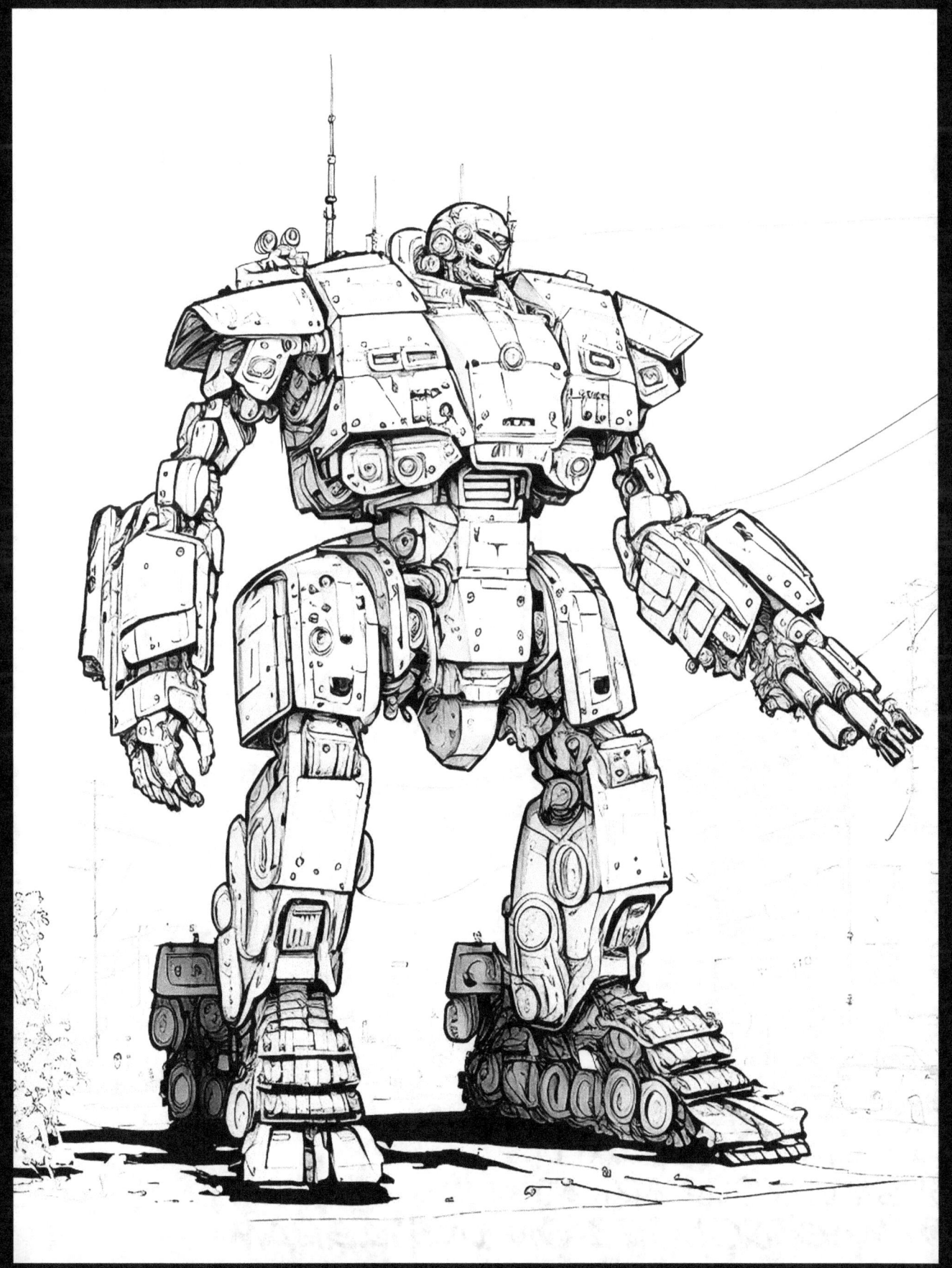

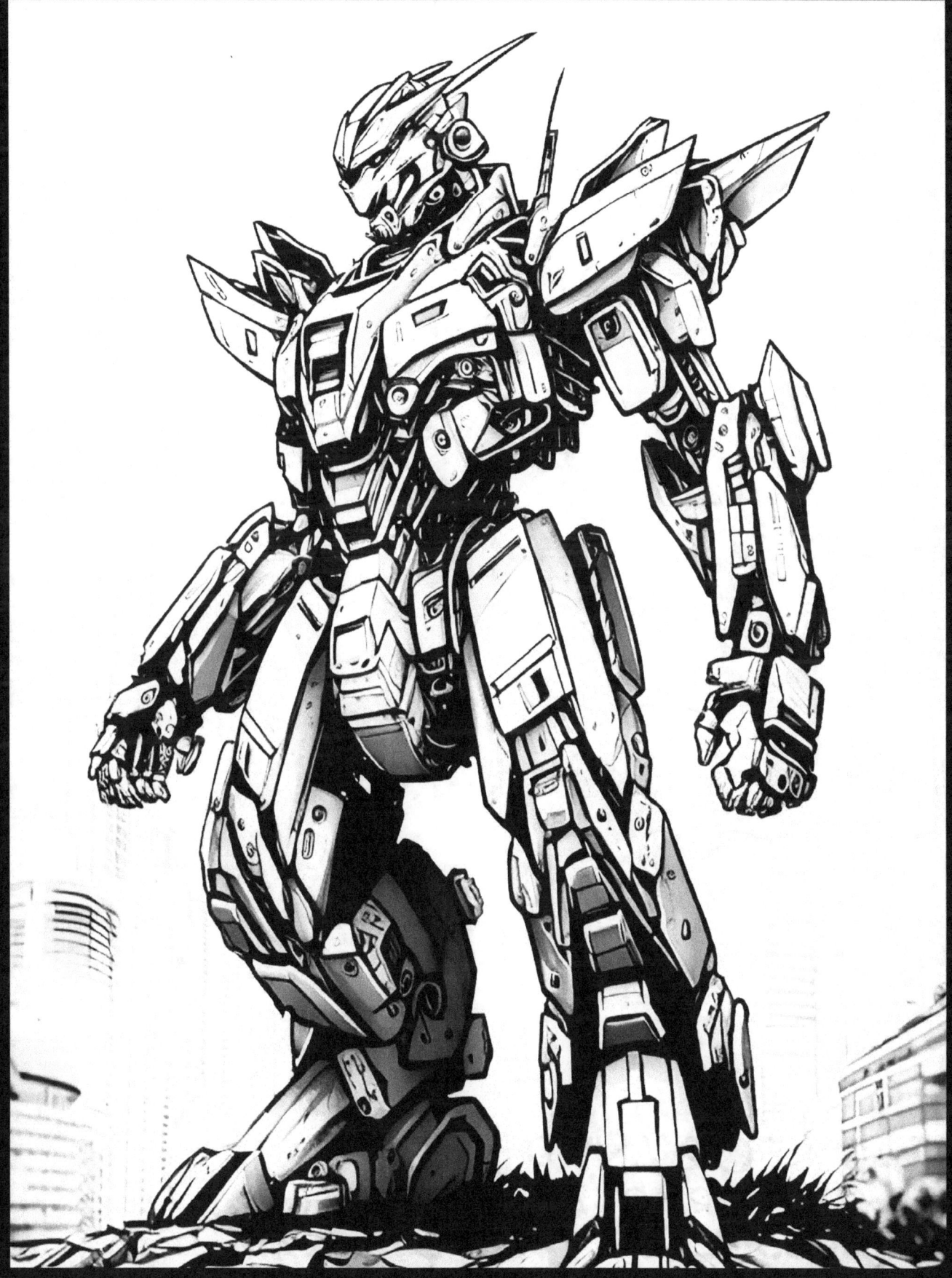

READY FOR ANYTHING
SUBMIT YOUR ART AT:
@IMAGICOLORZ ON INSTAGRAM

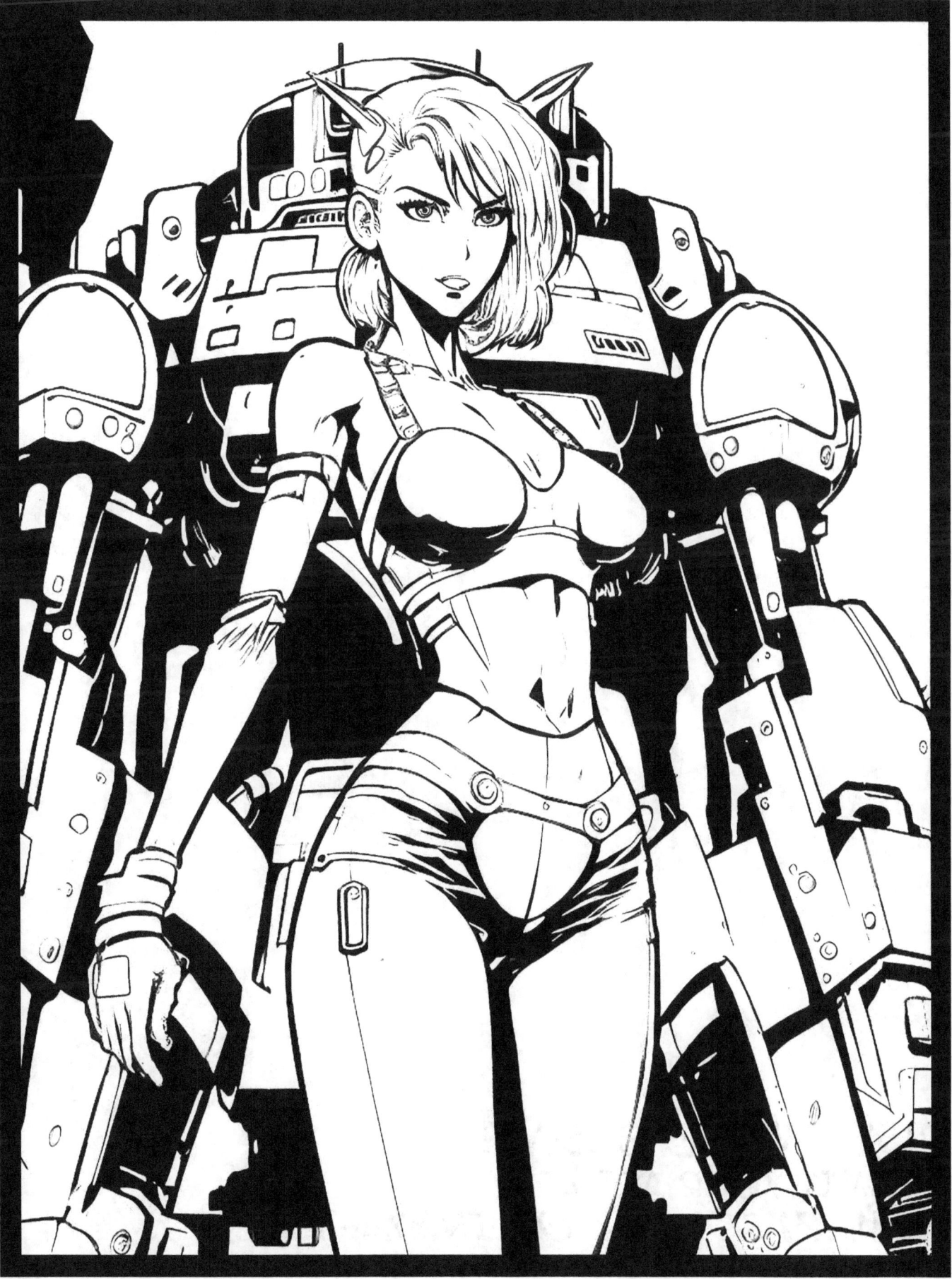

BOT IN THE SLUMS
SUBMIT YOUR ART AT:
@IMAGICOLORZ ON INSTAGRAM

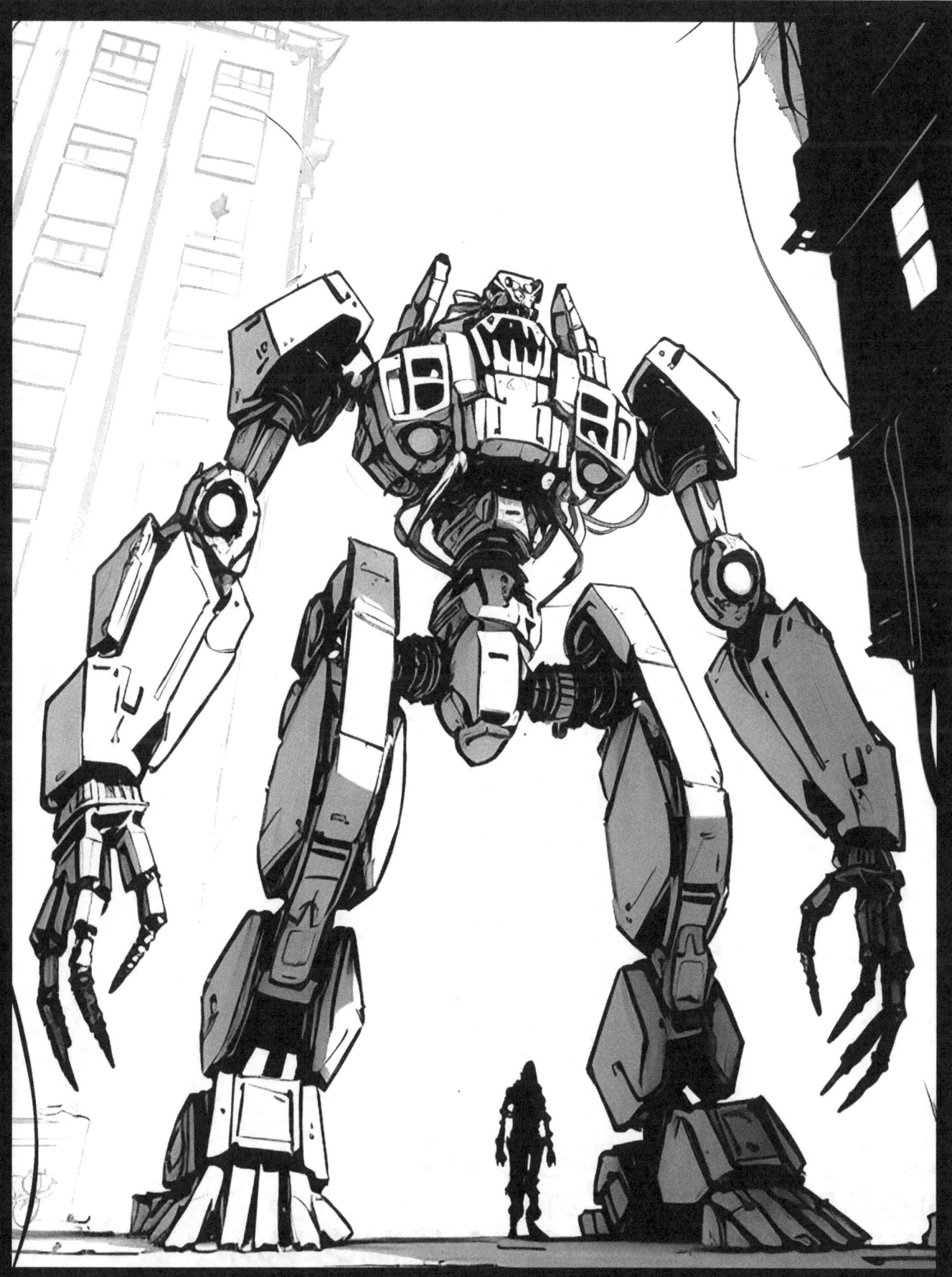

ARMORED WARRIORS
SUBMIT YOUR ART AT:
@IMAGICOLORZ ON INSTAGRAM

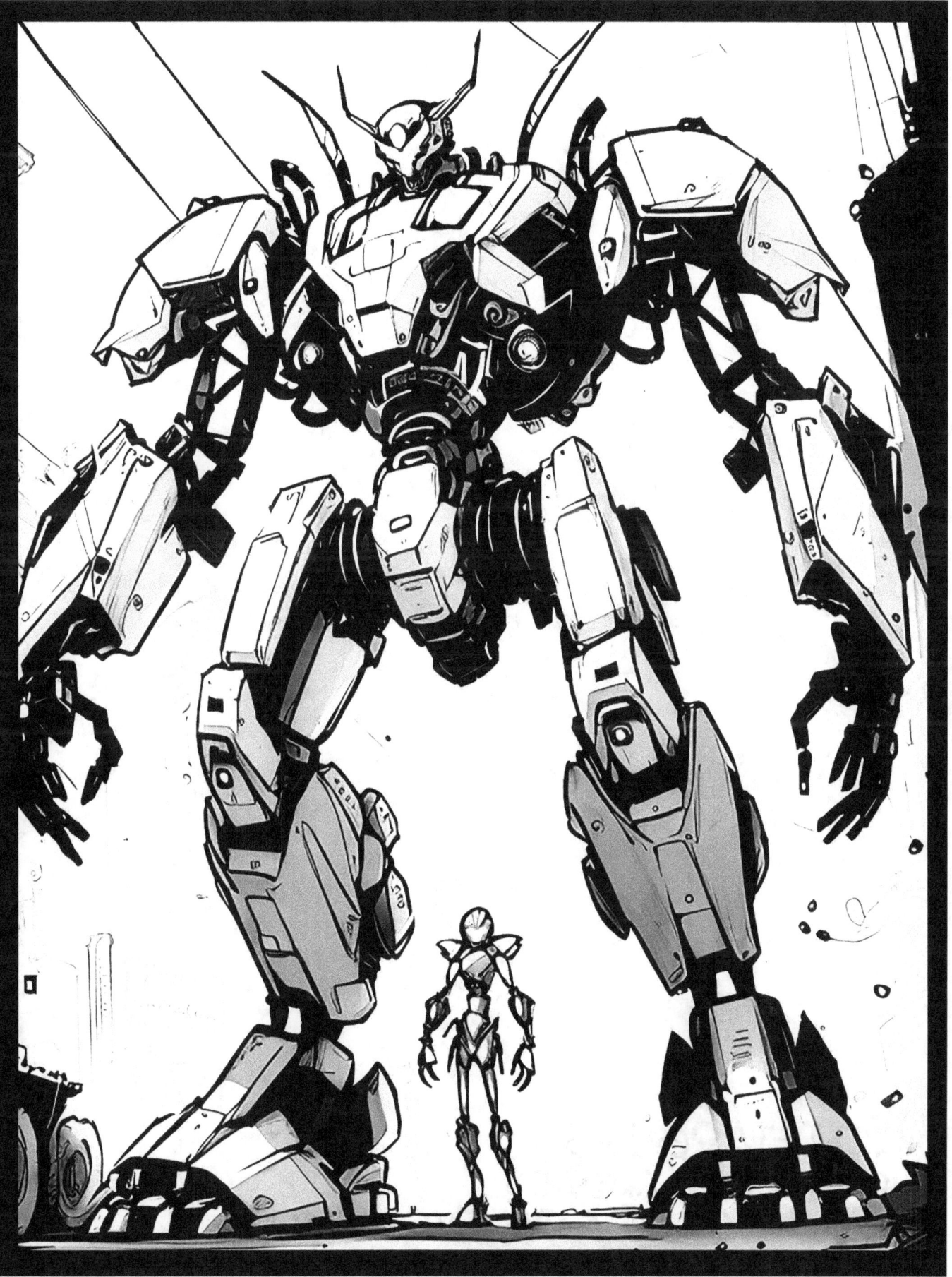

MULTI-TARGETS
SUBMIT YOUR ART AT:
@IMAGICOLORZ ON INSTAGRAM

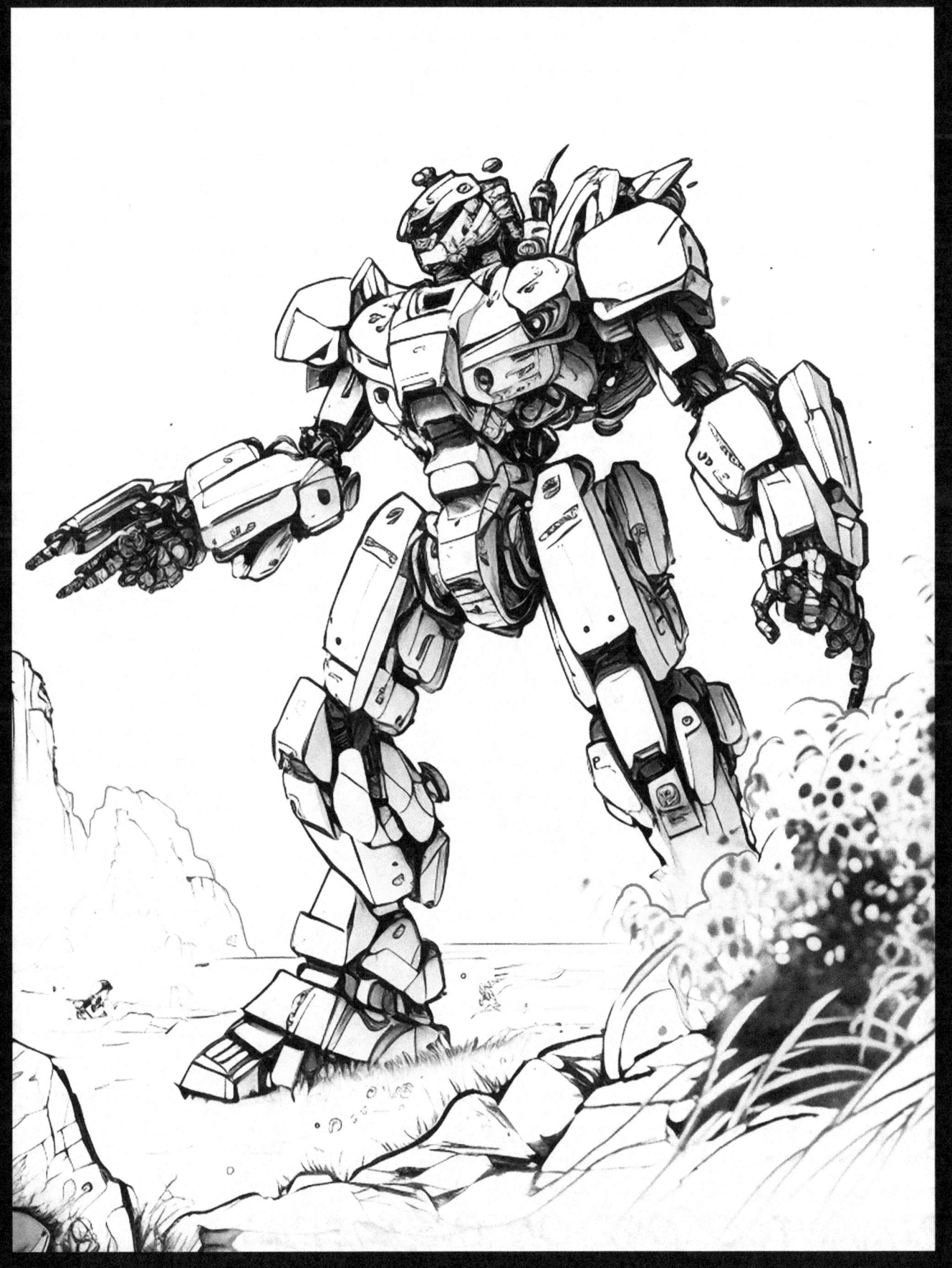

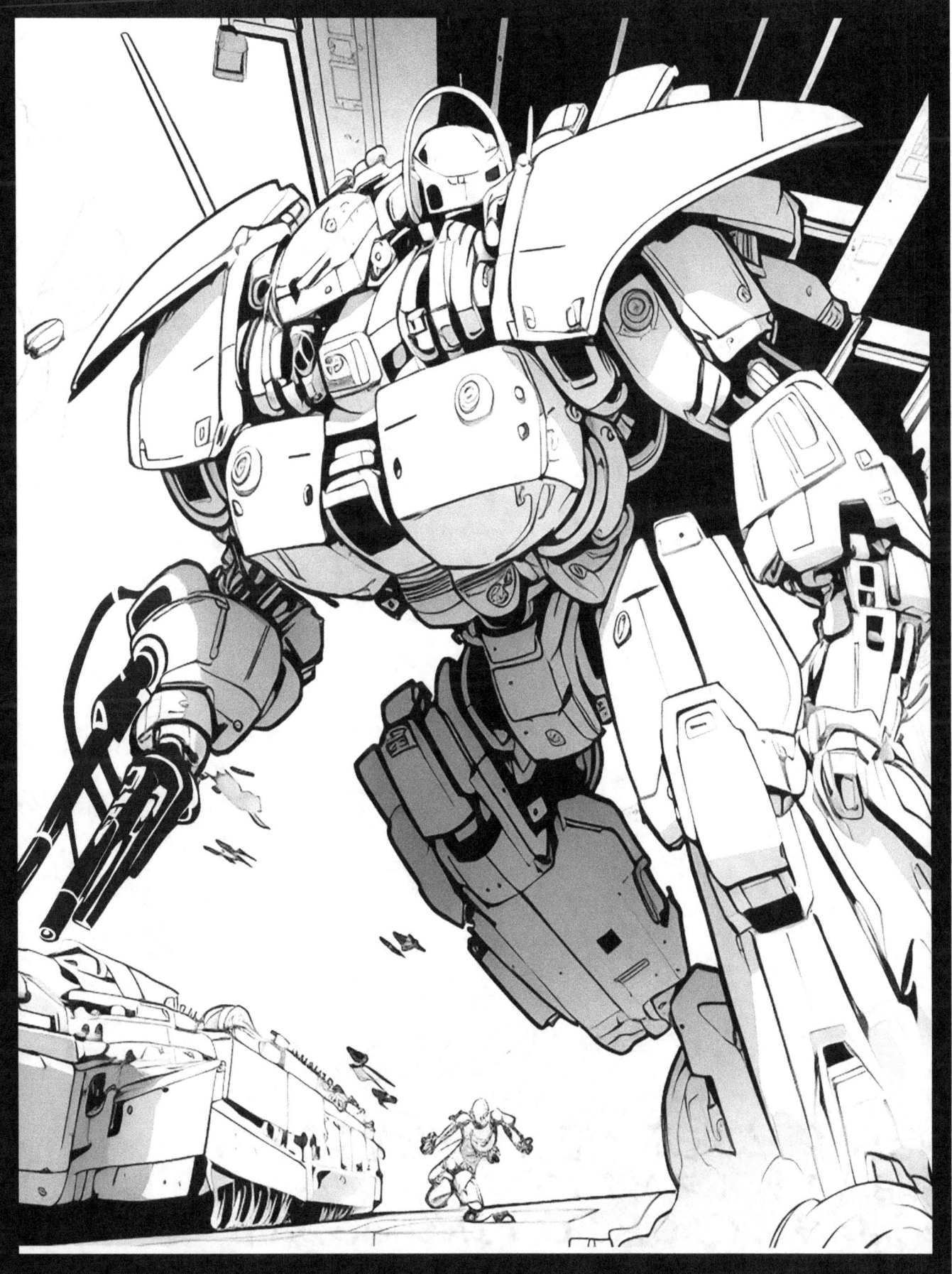

NEW PLANET, NEW ENEMIES
SUBMIT YOUR ART AT:
@IMAGICOLORZ ON INSTAGRAM

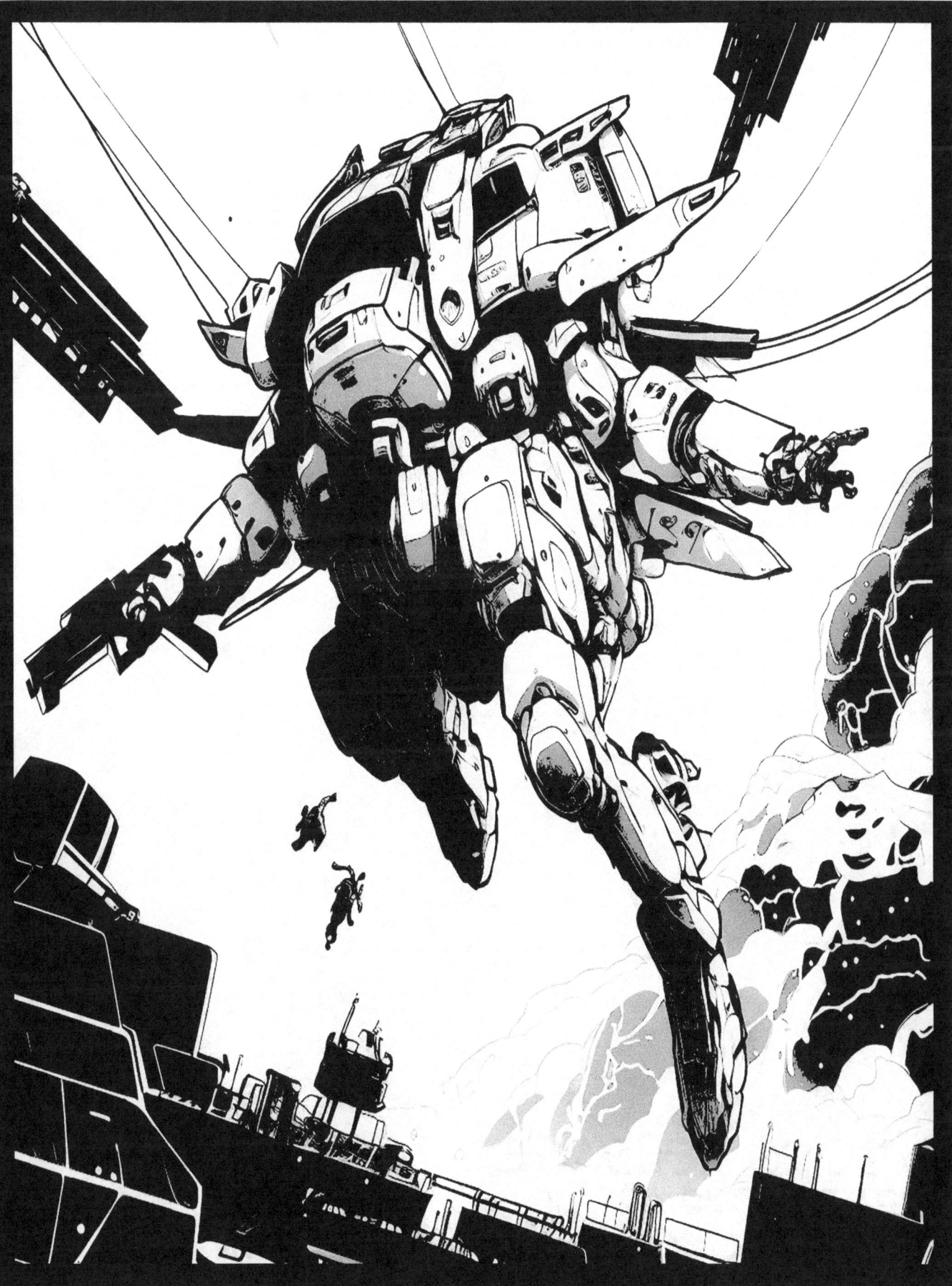

CYBORG RELEASE
SUBMIT YOUR ART AT:
@IMAGICOLORZ ON INSTAGRAM

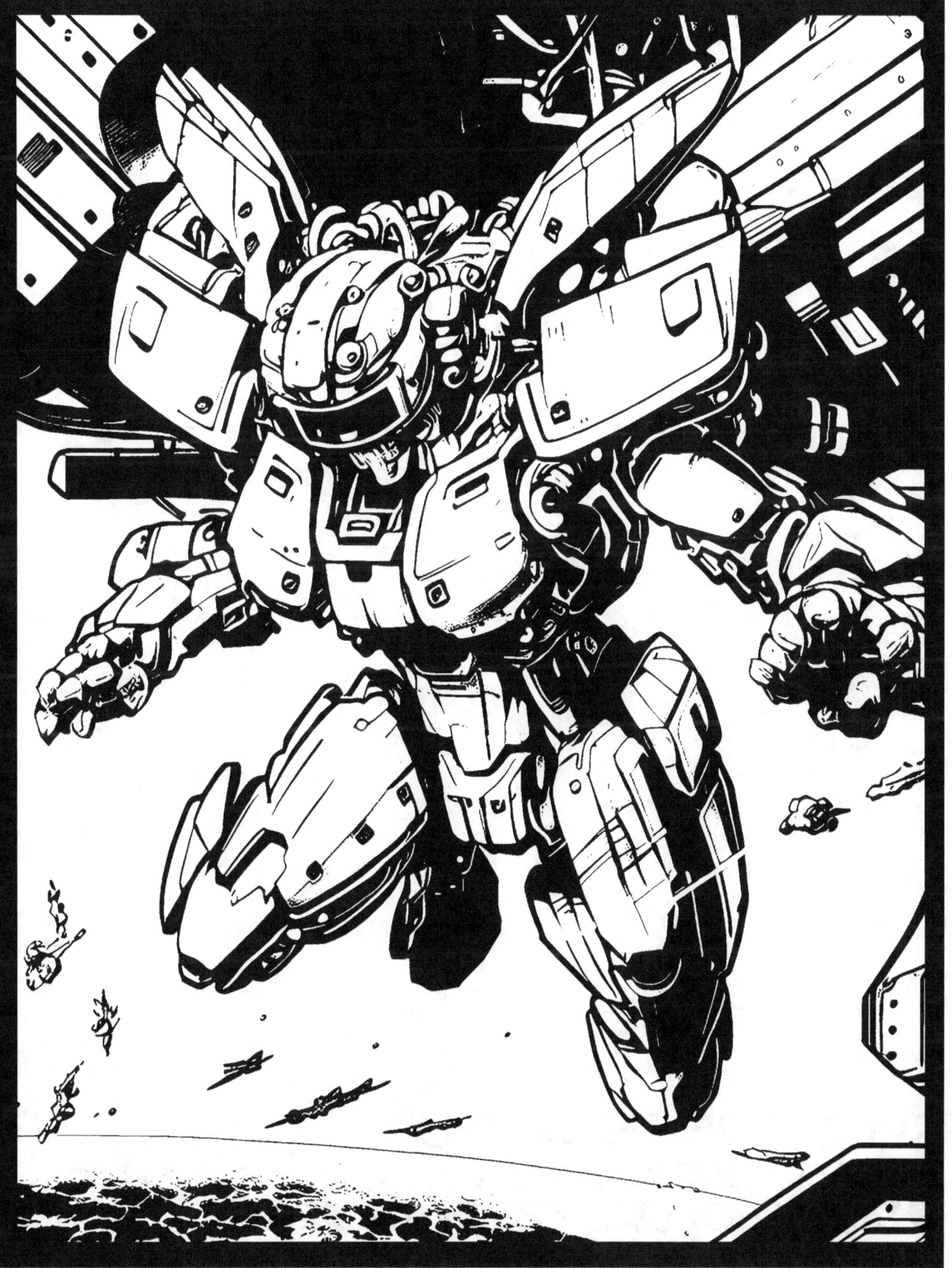

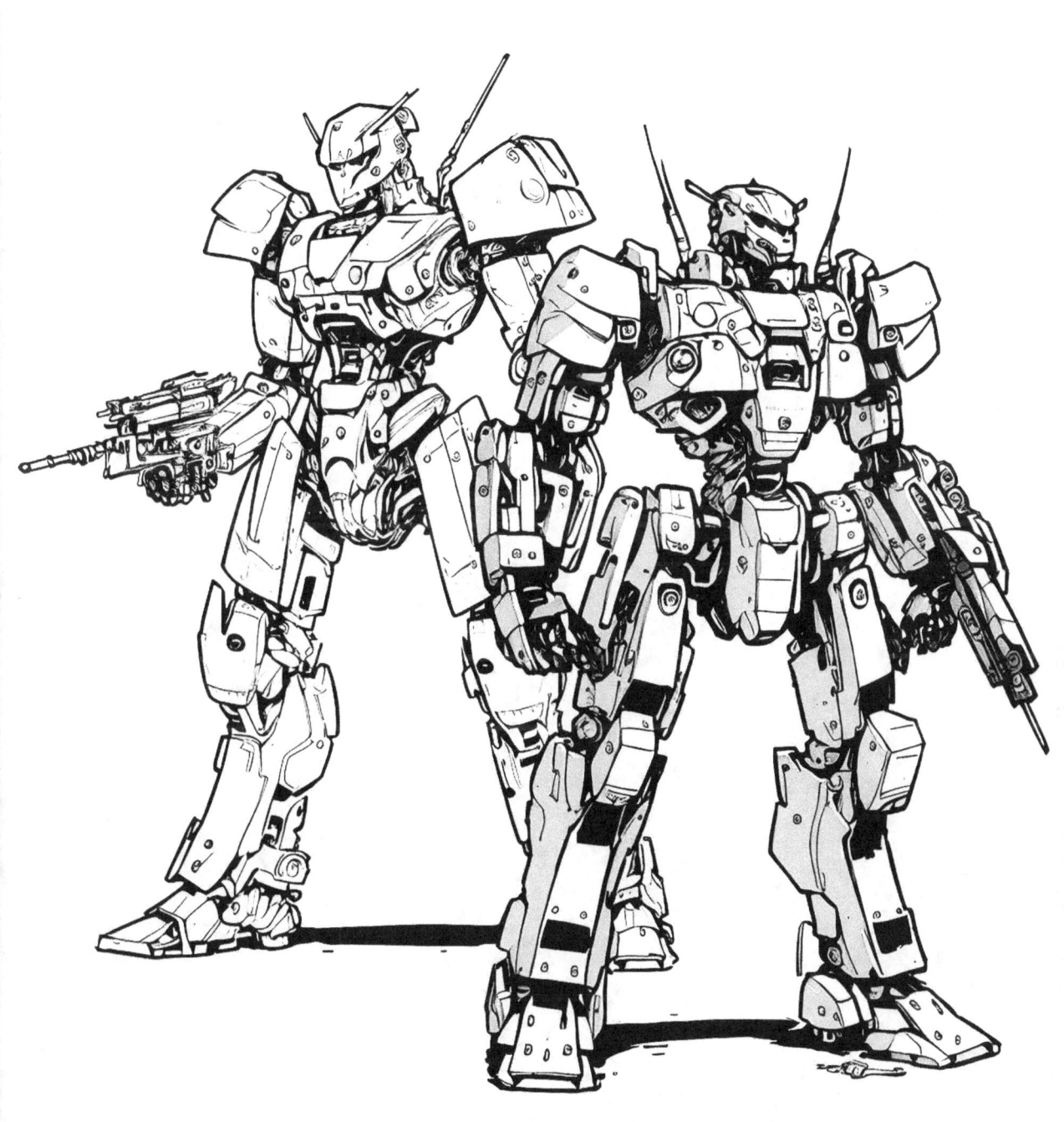

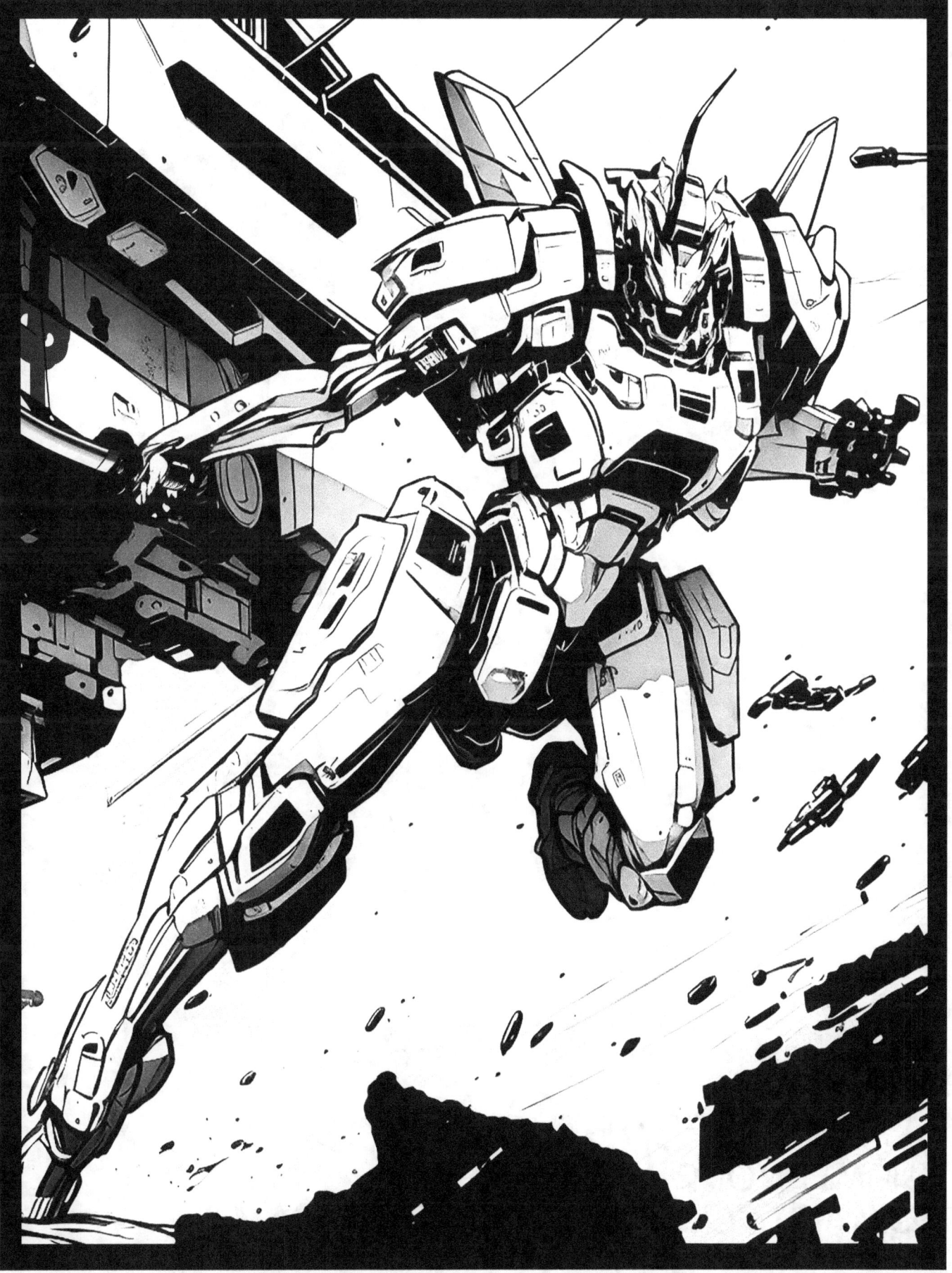

ALIEN DEFENSIVE FORCE
SUBMIT YOUR ART AT:
@IMAGICOLORZ ON INSTAGRAM

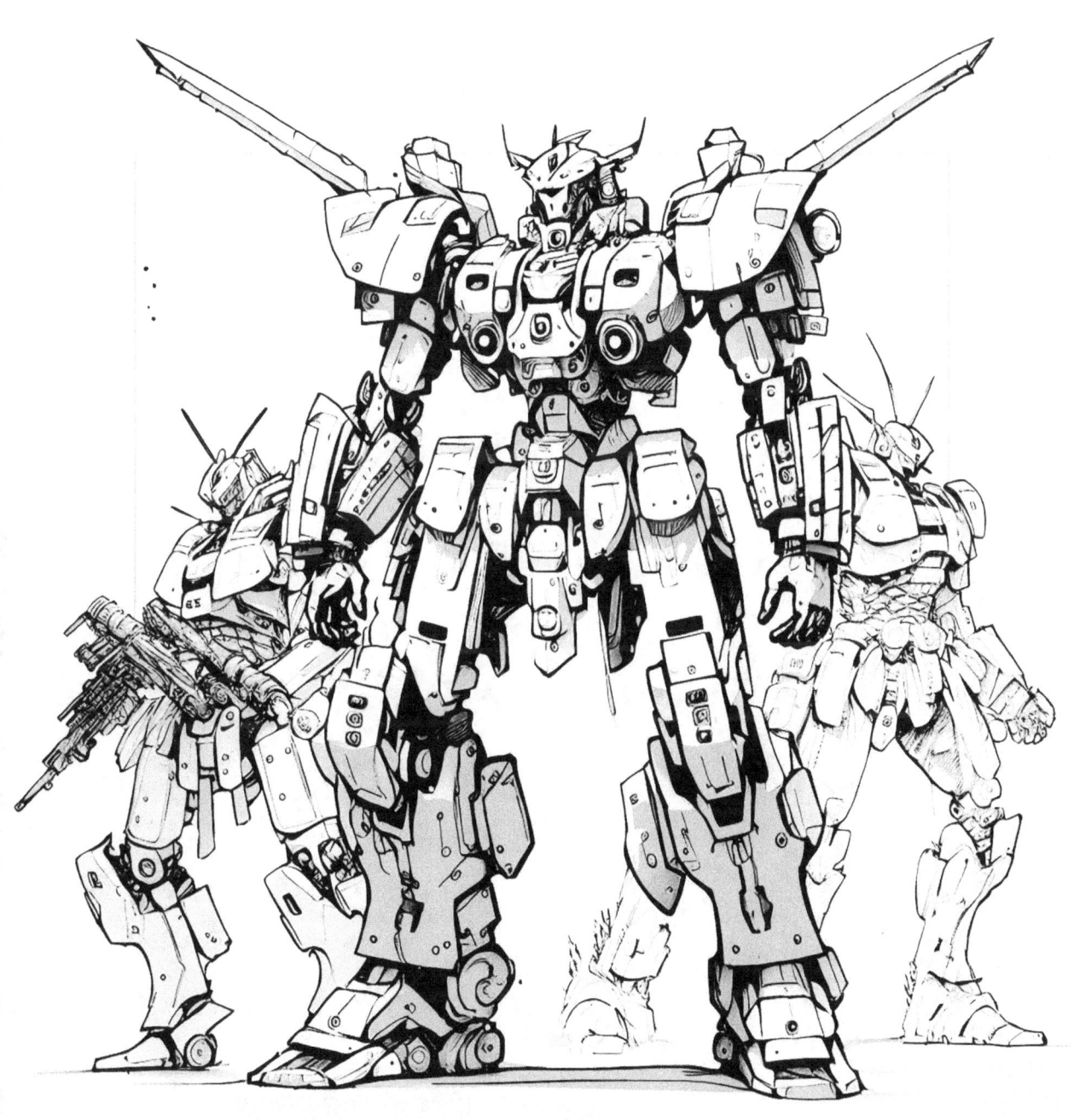

BEEP BEETLE
SUBMIT YOUR ART AT:
@IMAGICOLORZ ON INSTAGRAM

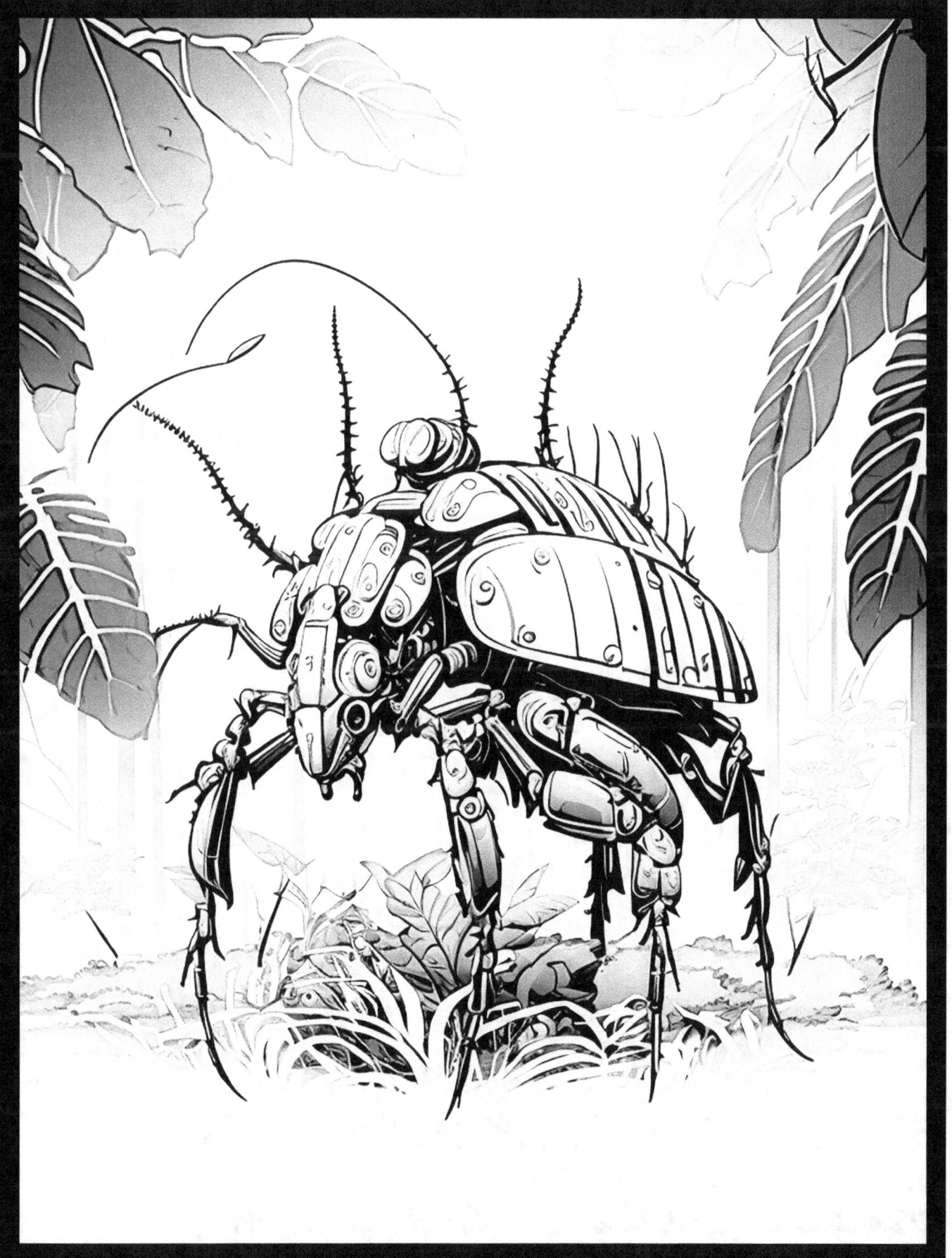

STEAM PUNK JUNK HARVESTER
SUBMIT YOUR ART AT:
@IMAGICOLORZ ON INSTAGRAM

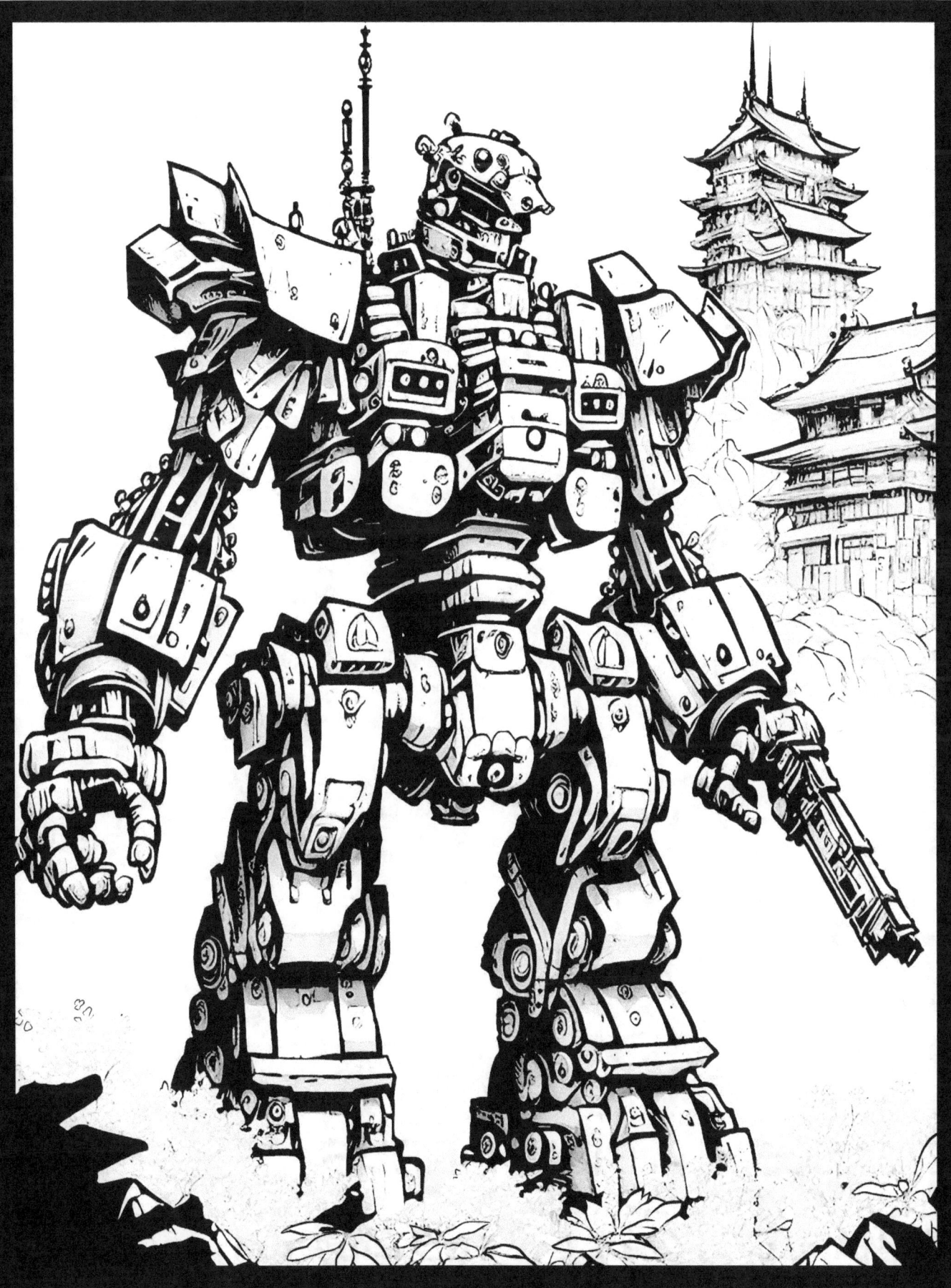

BATTLESHIP DRAGONEUS
SUBMIT YOUR ART AT:
@IMAGICOLORZ ON INSTAGRAM

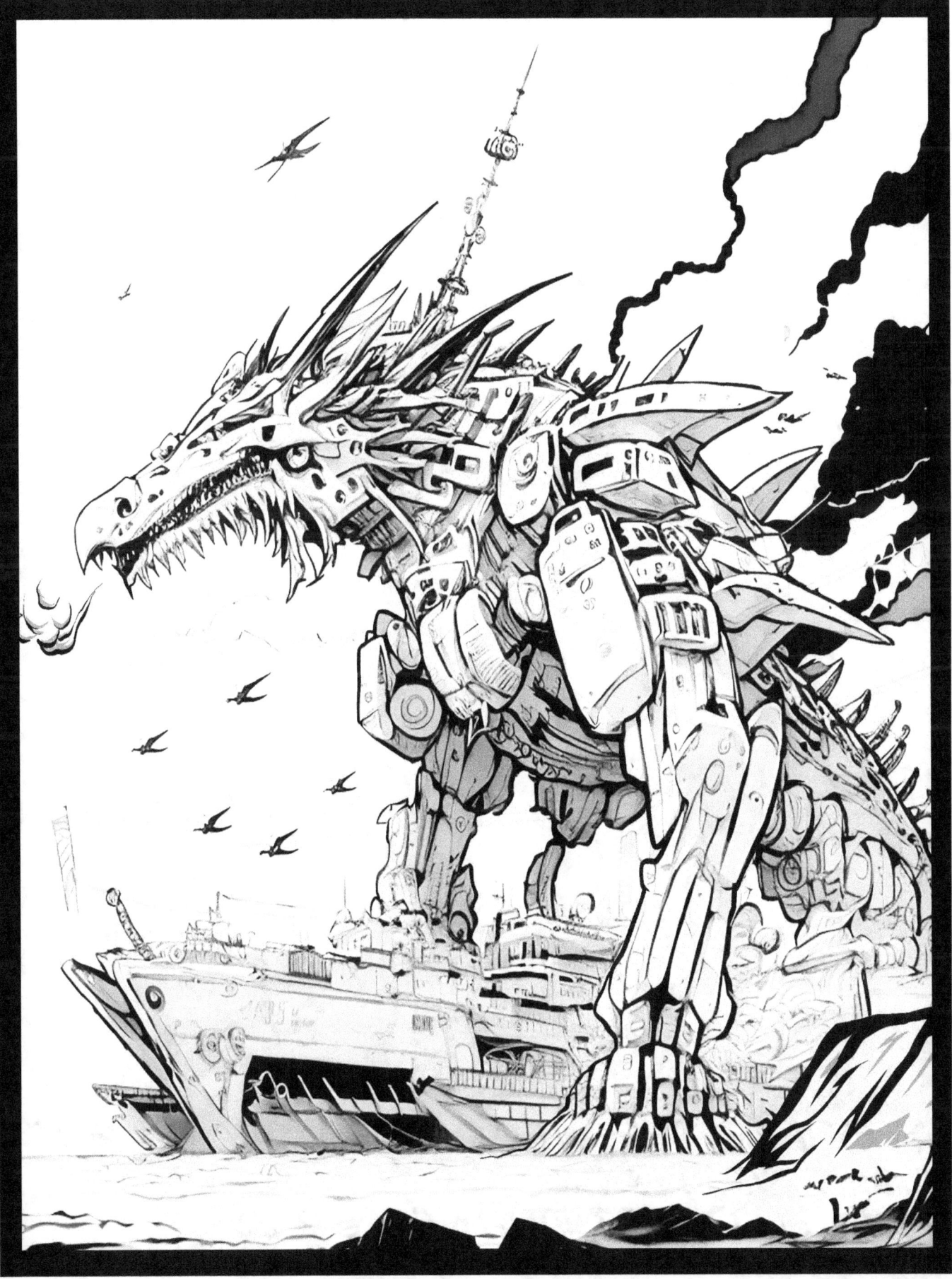

IN SPACE THE WEAPONS ARE SILENT
SUBMIT YOUR ART AT:
@IMAGICOLORZ ON INSTAGRAM

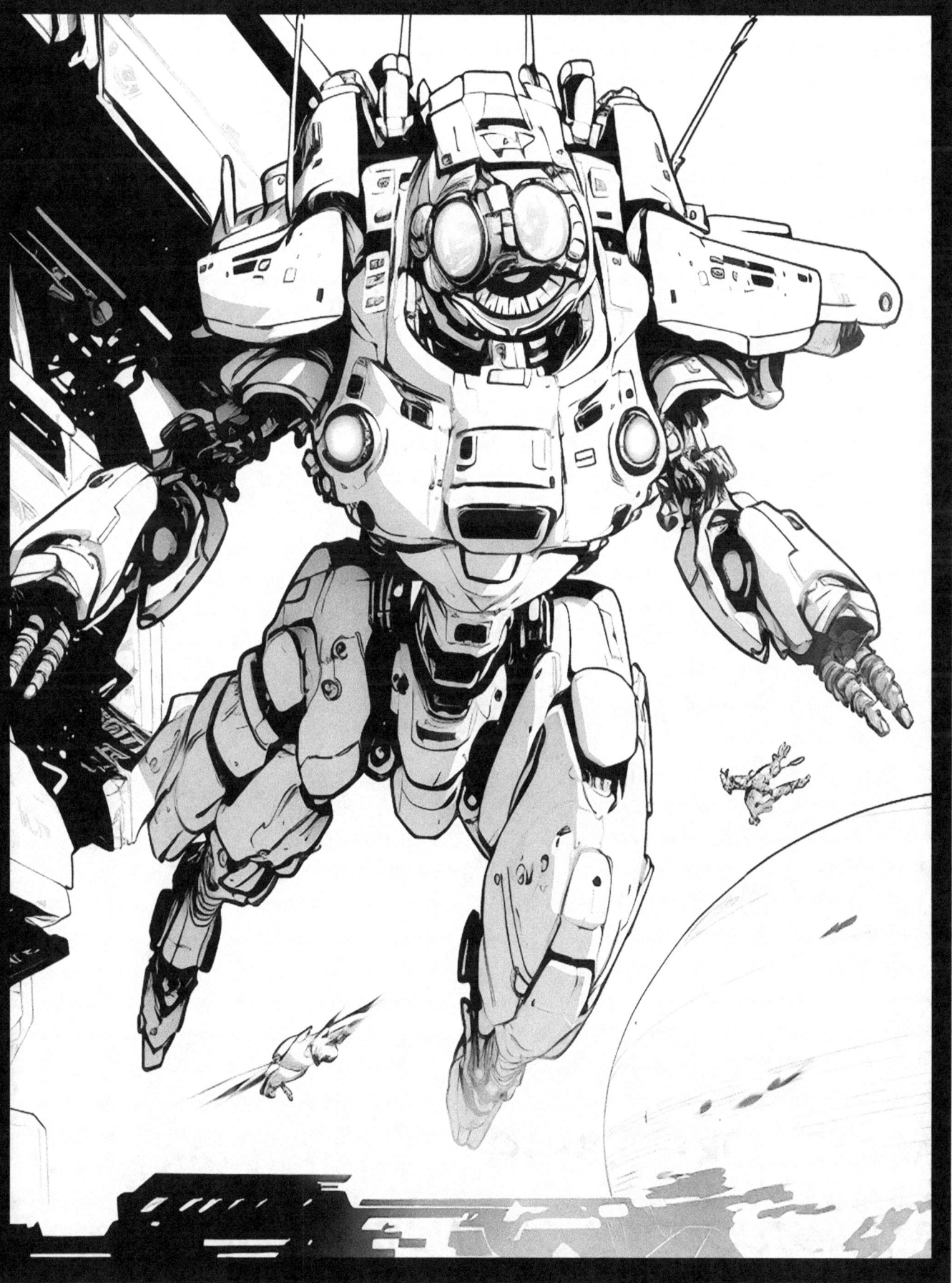

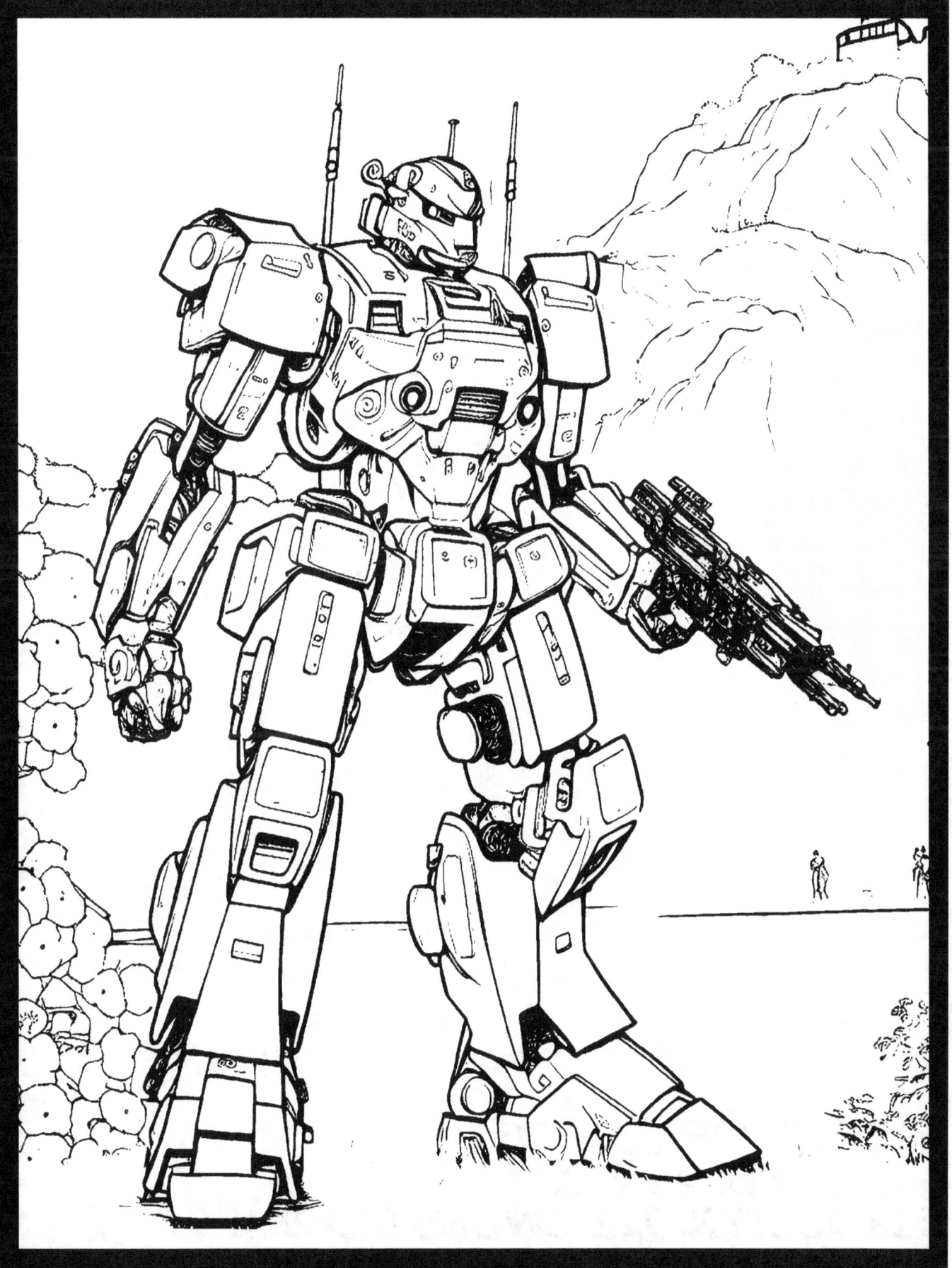

FLIGHT OF BATTLE

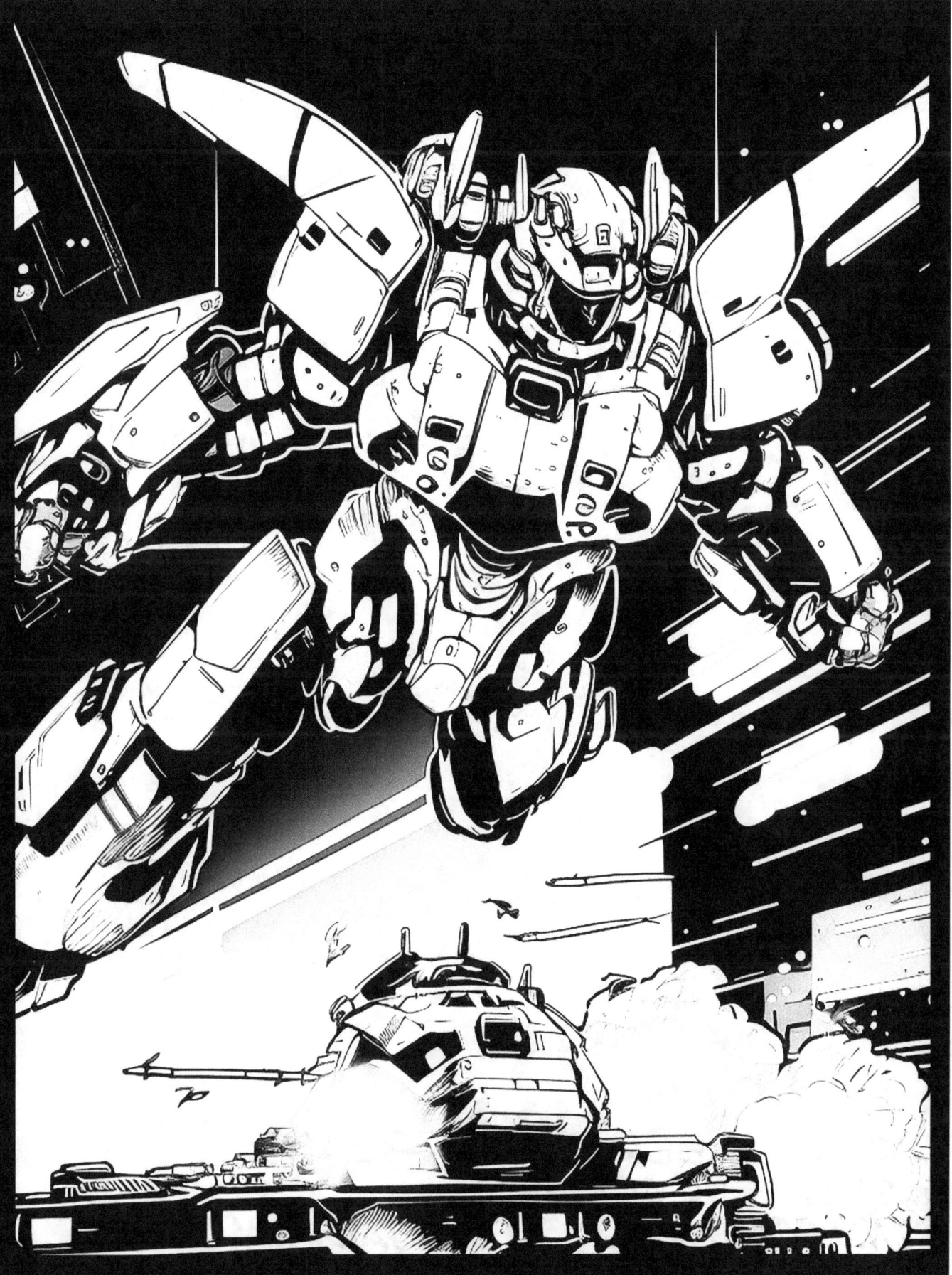

LAZER SABER WRIST BLADE
SUBMIT YOUR ART AT:
@IMAGICOLORZ ON INSTAGRAM

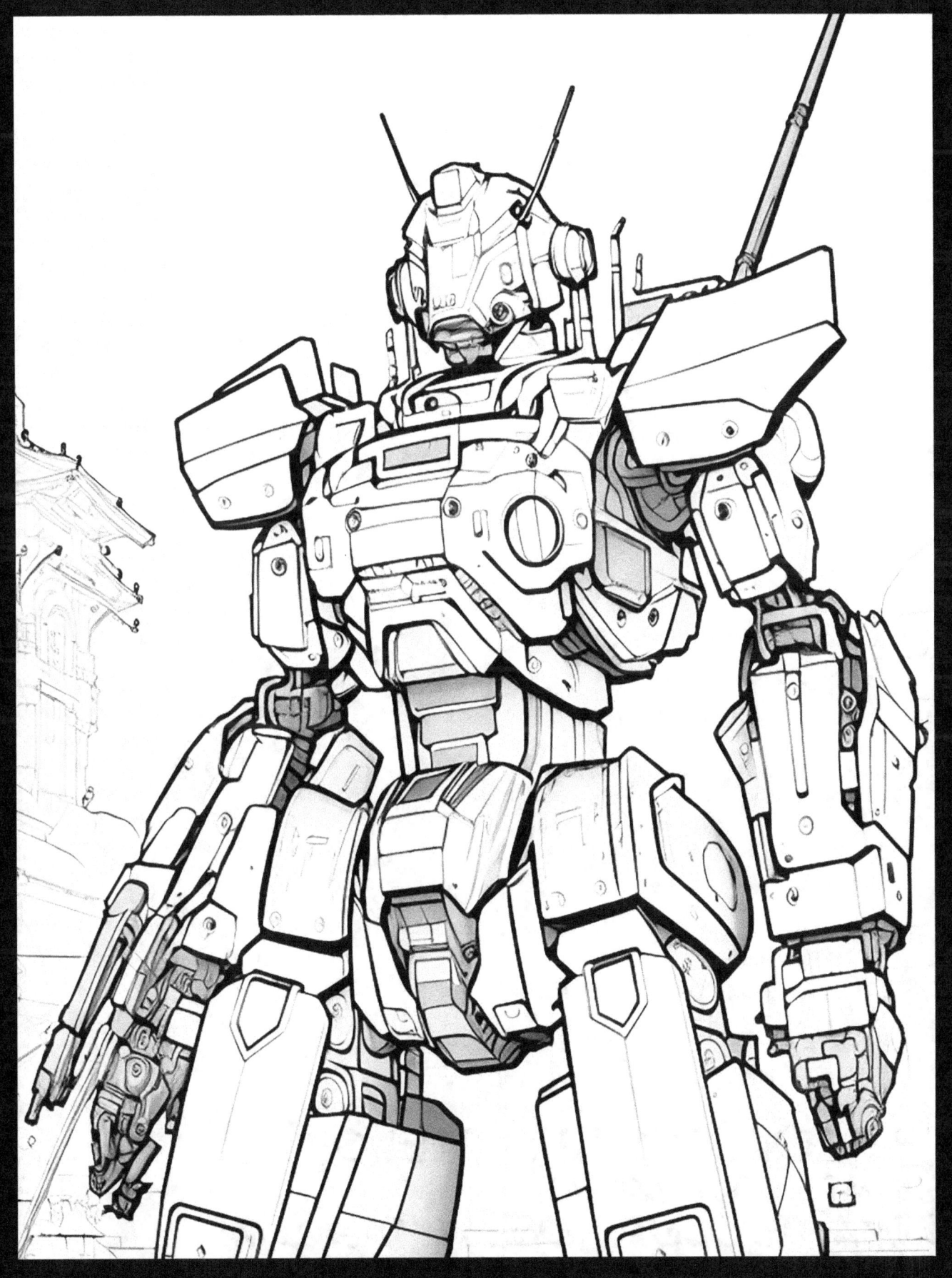

THE COLLECTOR'S FIELD
SUBMIT YOUR ART AT:
@IMAGICOLORZ ON INSTAGRAM

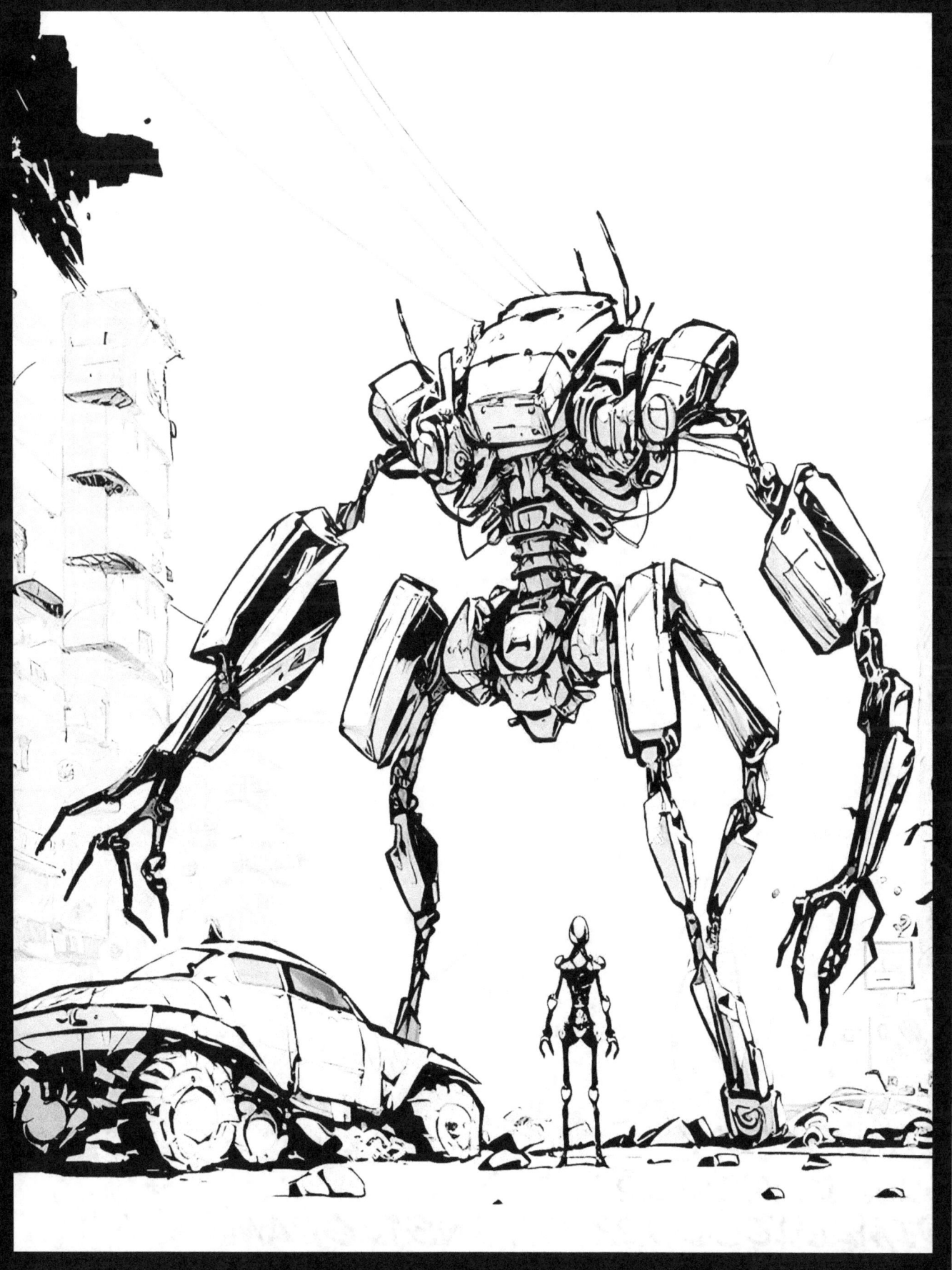

CAMO-SPY
SUBMIT YOUR ART AT:
@IMAGICOLORZ ON INSTAGRAM

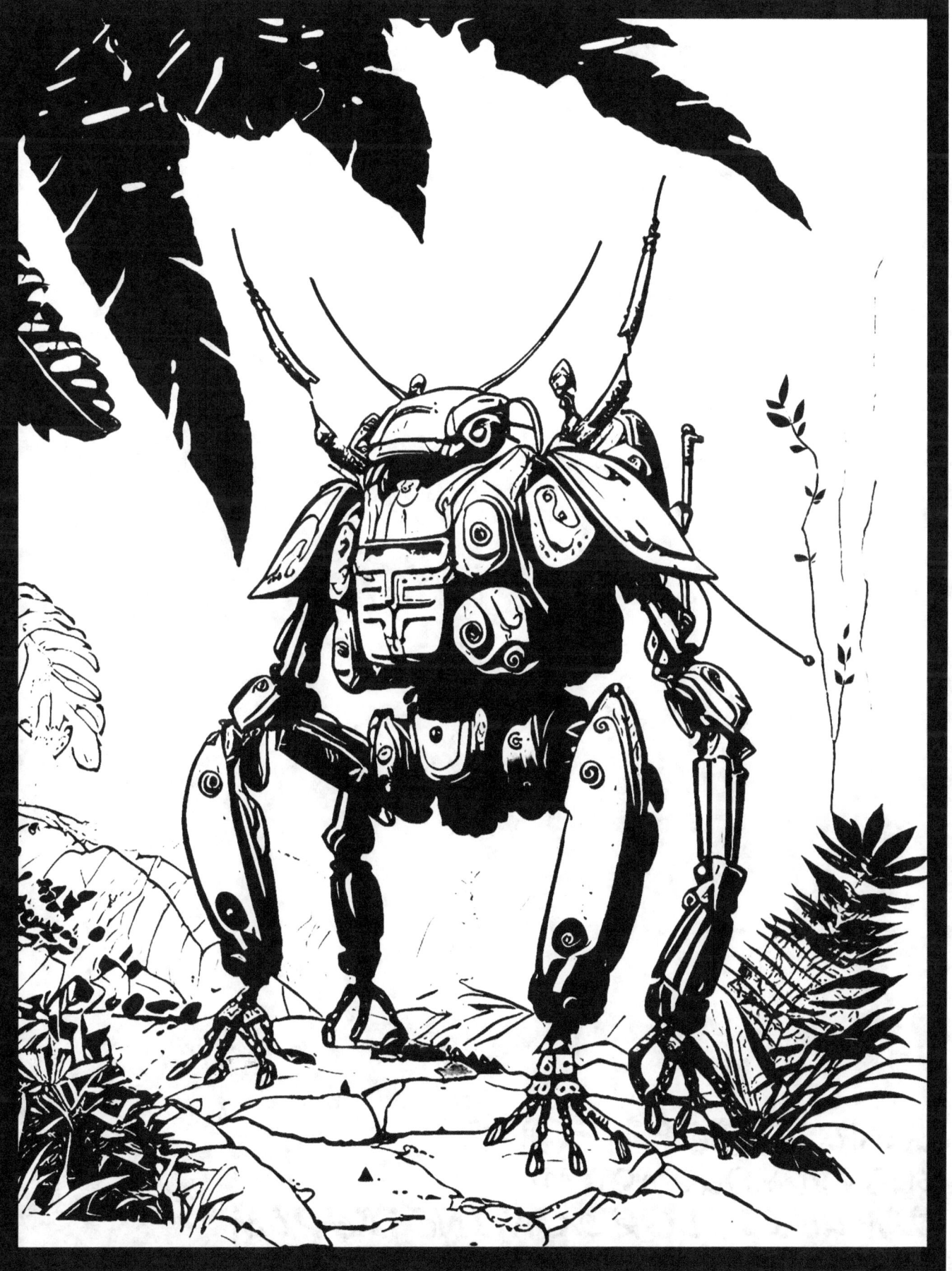

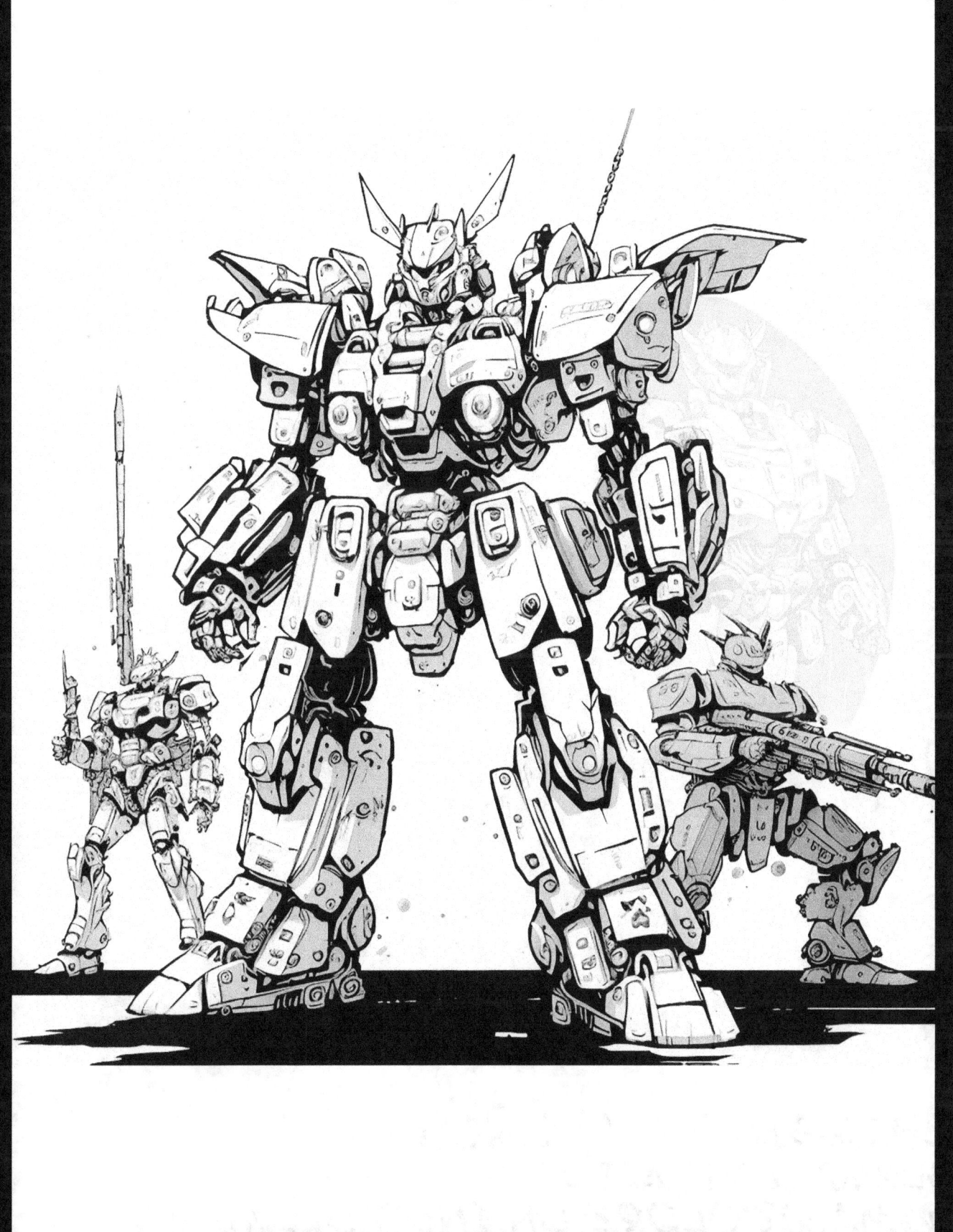

CHARGING MY PUNCH!
SUBMIT YOUR ART AT:
@IMAGICOLORZ ON INSTAGRAM

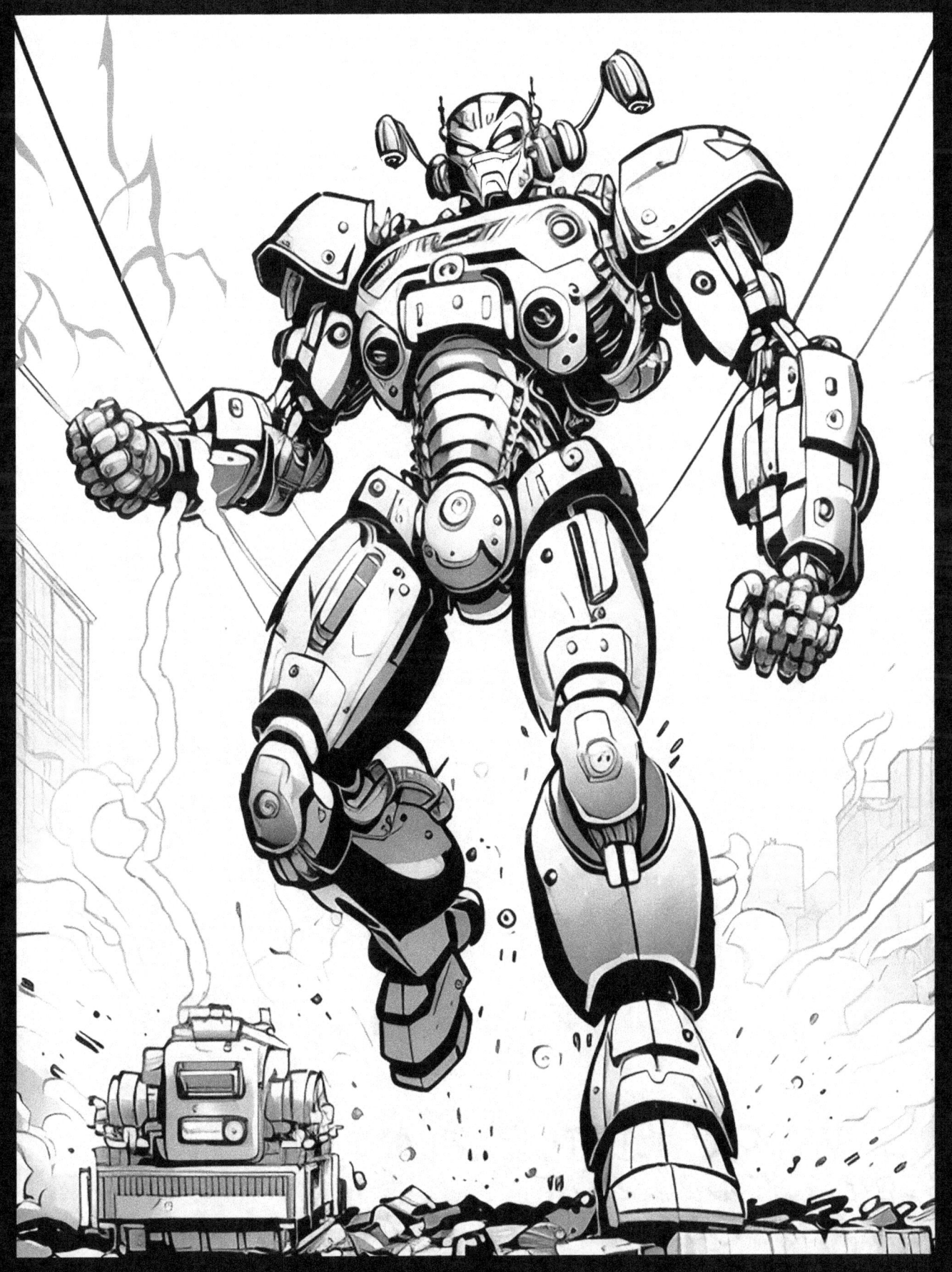

ALL WORK, LITTLE PLAY
SUBMIT YOUR ART AT:
@IMAGICOLORZ ON INSTAGRAM

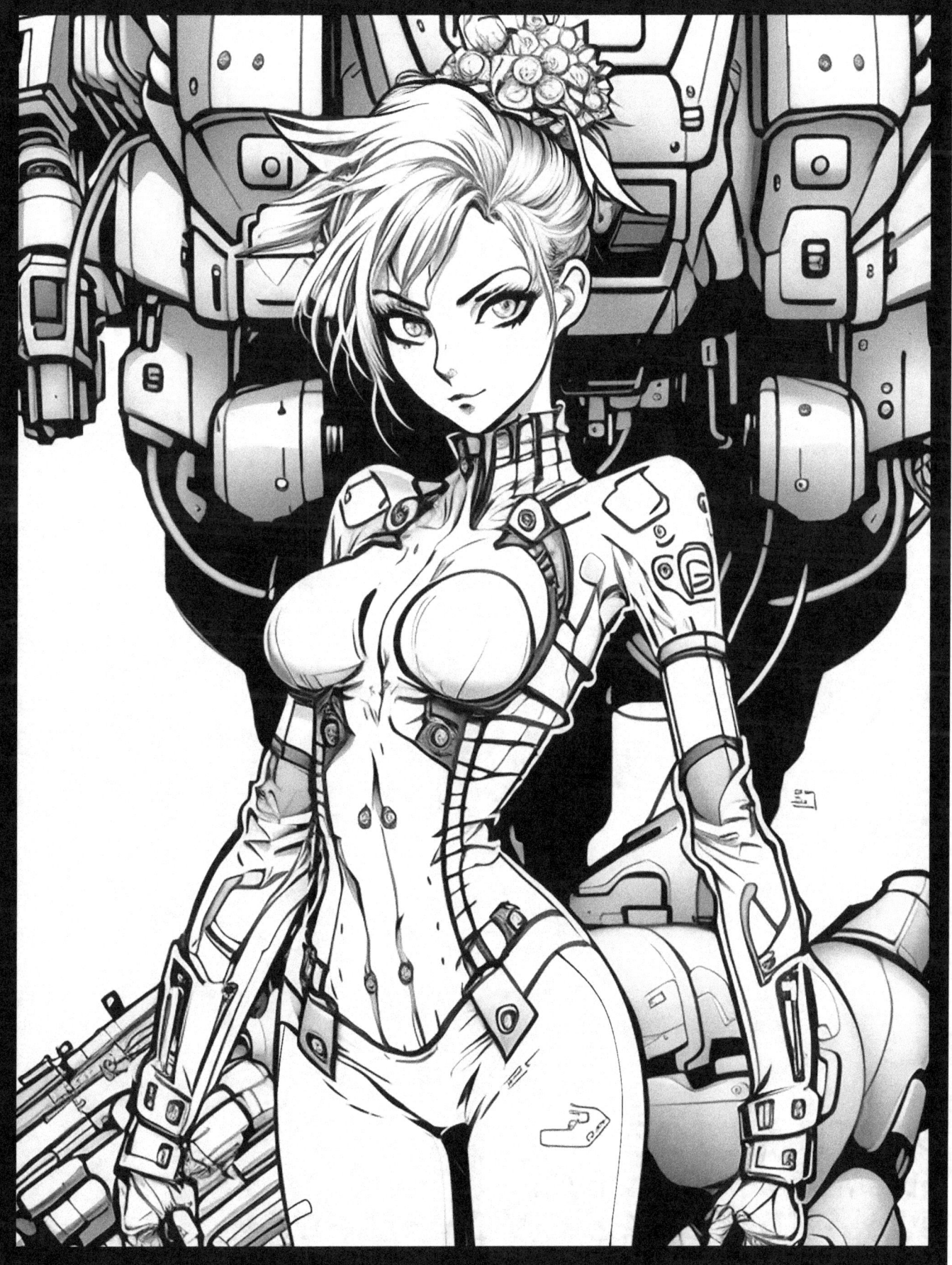

DEATH SLIDE
SUBMIT YOUR ART AT:
@IMAGICOLORZ ON INSTAGRAM

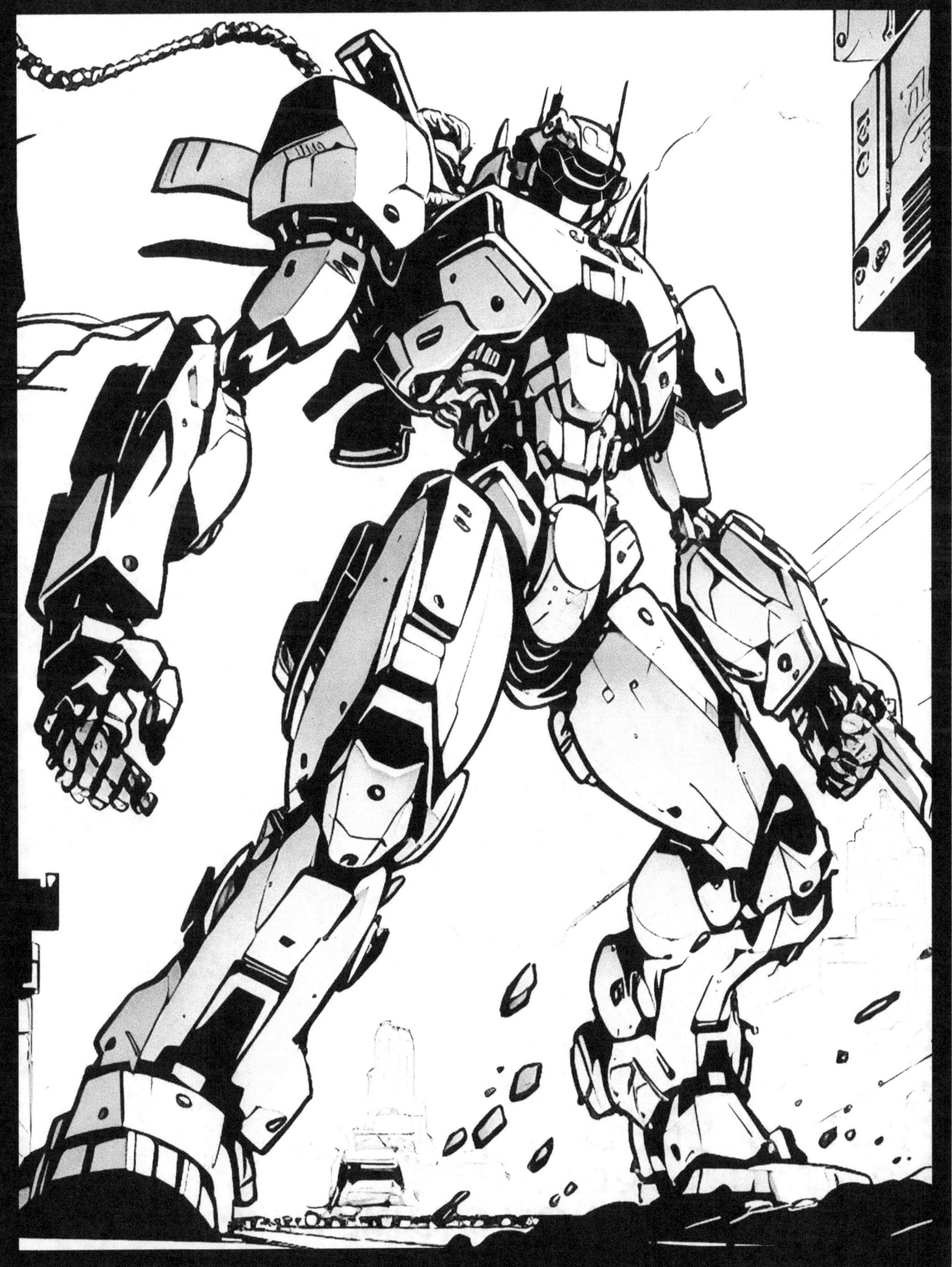

PILOT NEEDED
SUBMIT YOUR ART AT:
@IMAGICOLORZ ON INSTAGRAM

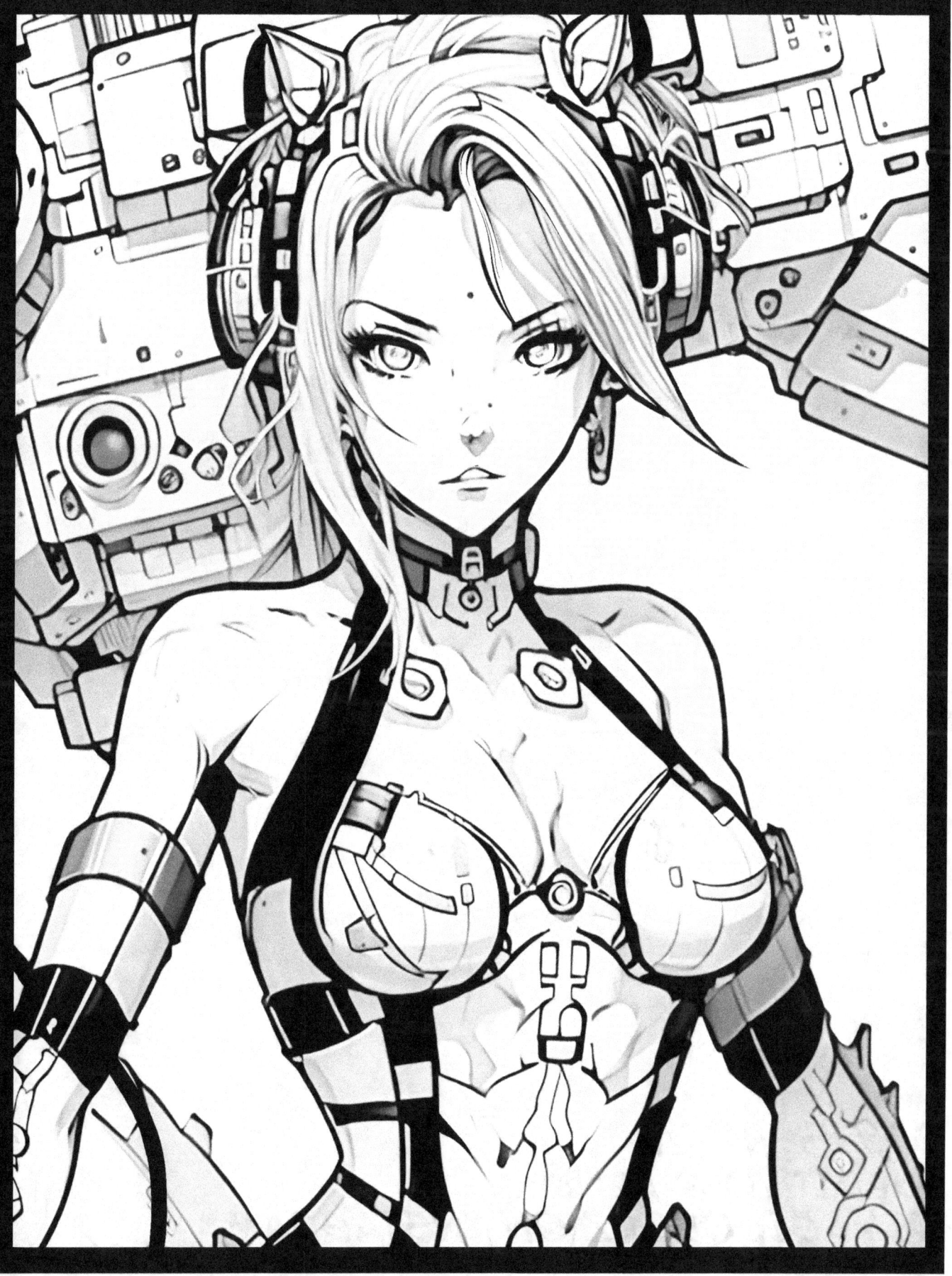

DAY'S WORK
SUBMIT YOUR ART AT:
@IMAGICOLORZ ON INSTAGRAM

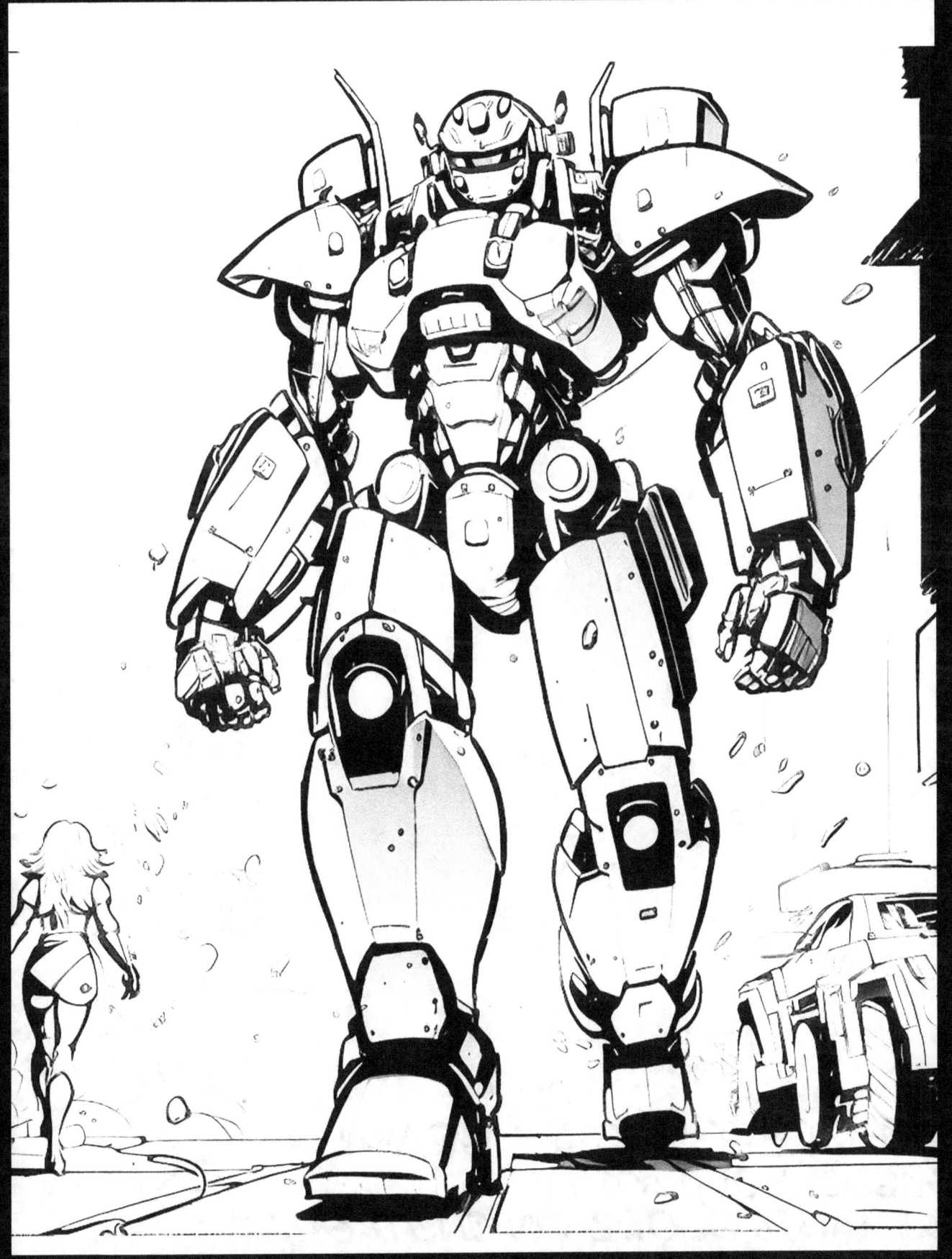

BEFORE THE CITY BRAWL
SUBMIT YOUR ART AT:
@IMAGICOLORZ ON INSTAGRAM

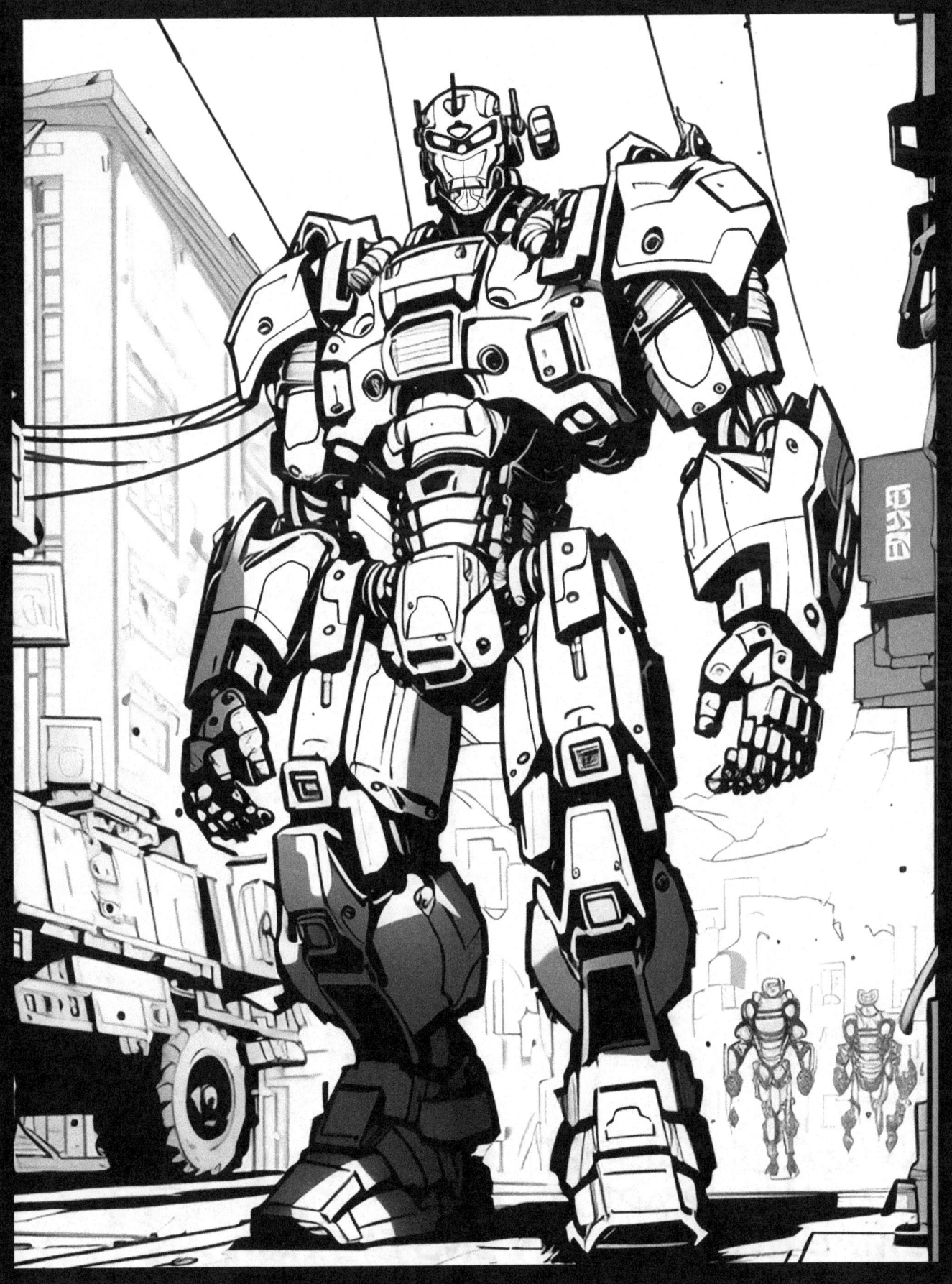

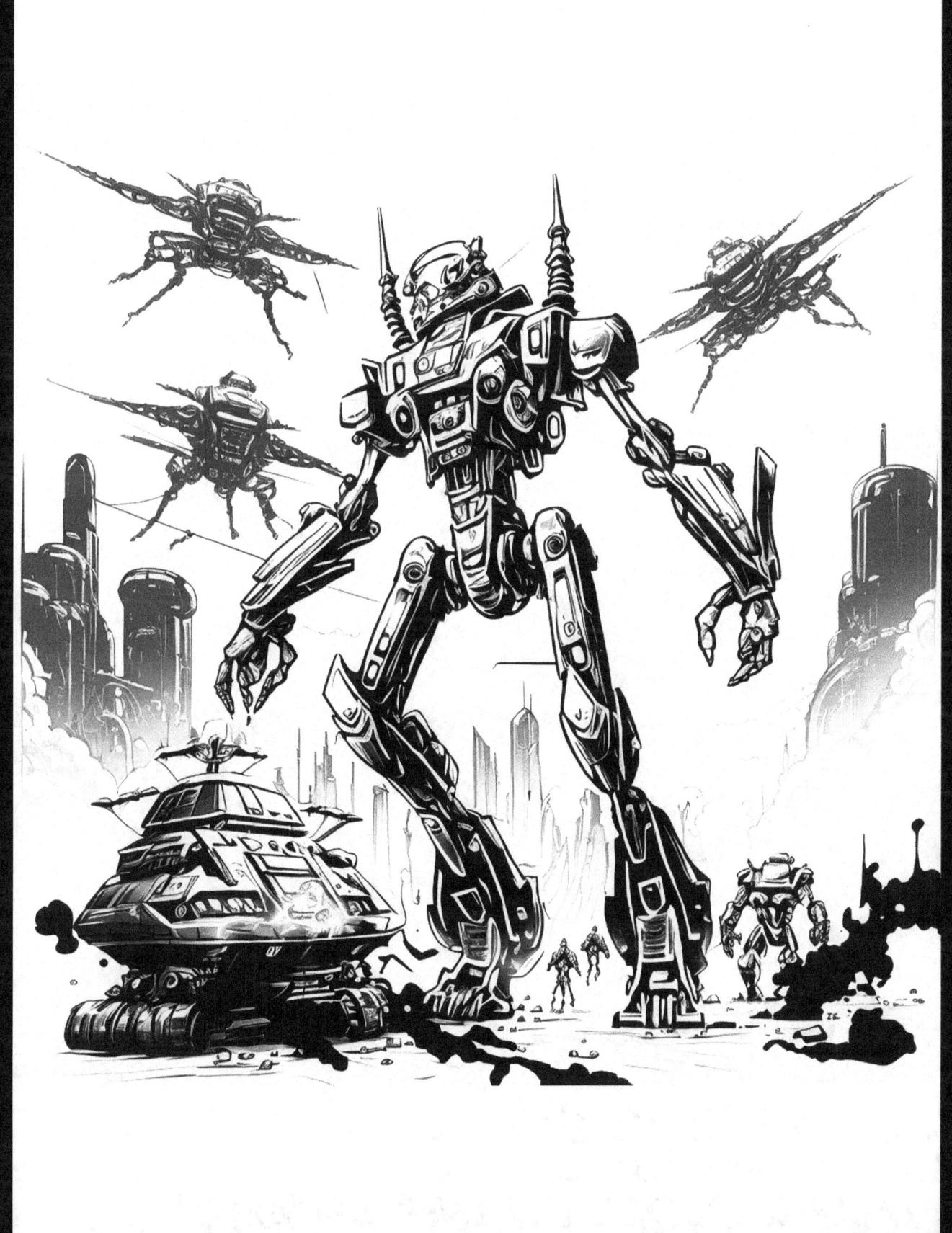

ALL SYSTEMS GO
SUBMIT YOUR ART AT:
@IMAGICOLORZ ON INSTAGRAM

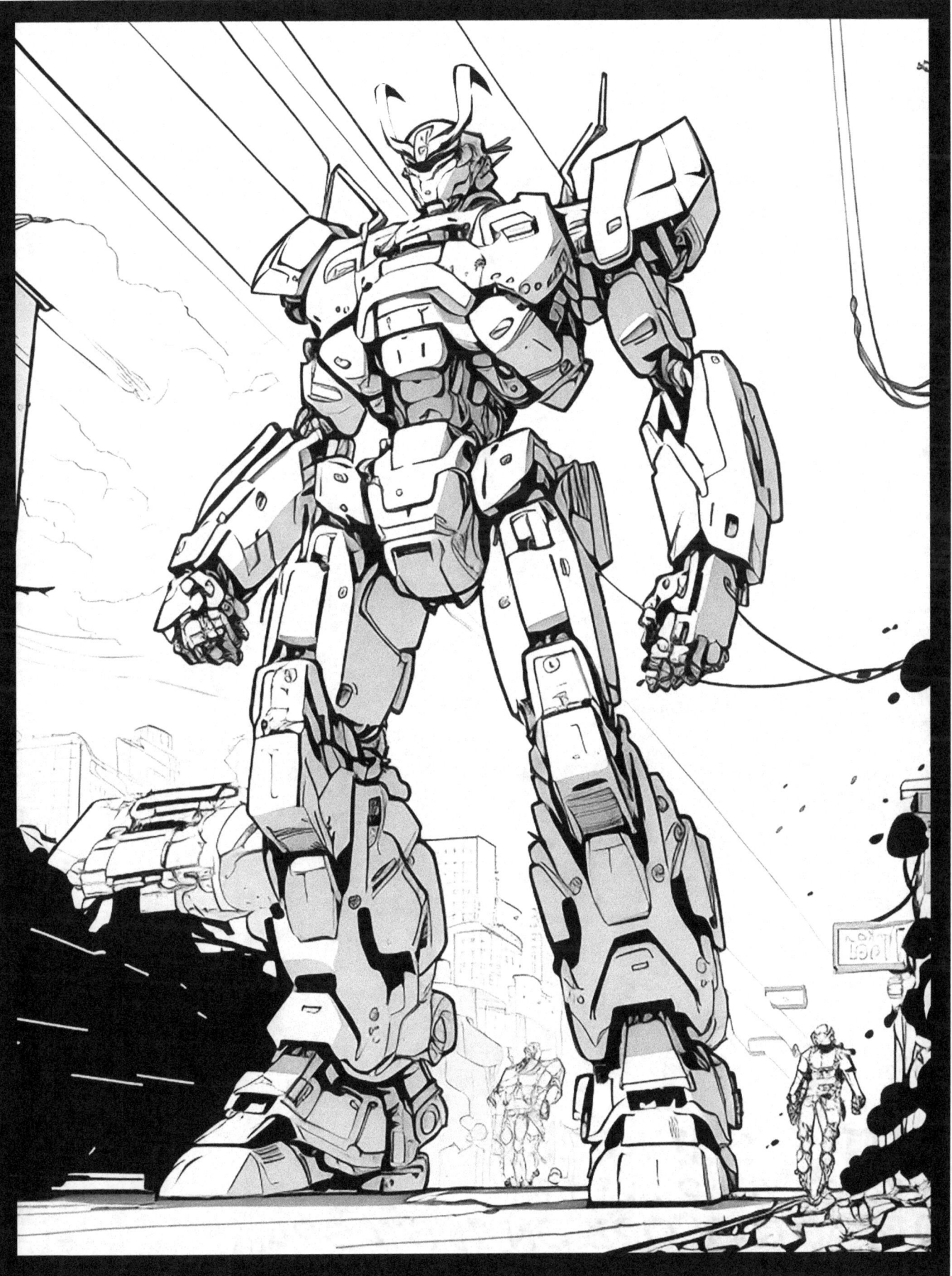

BATTLE SUIT READY
SUBMIT YOUR ART AT:
@IMAGICOLORZ ON INSTAGRAM

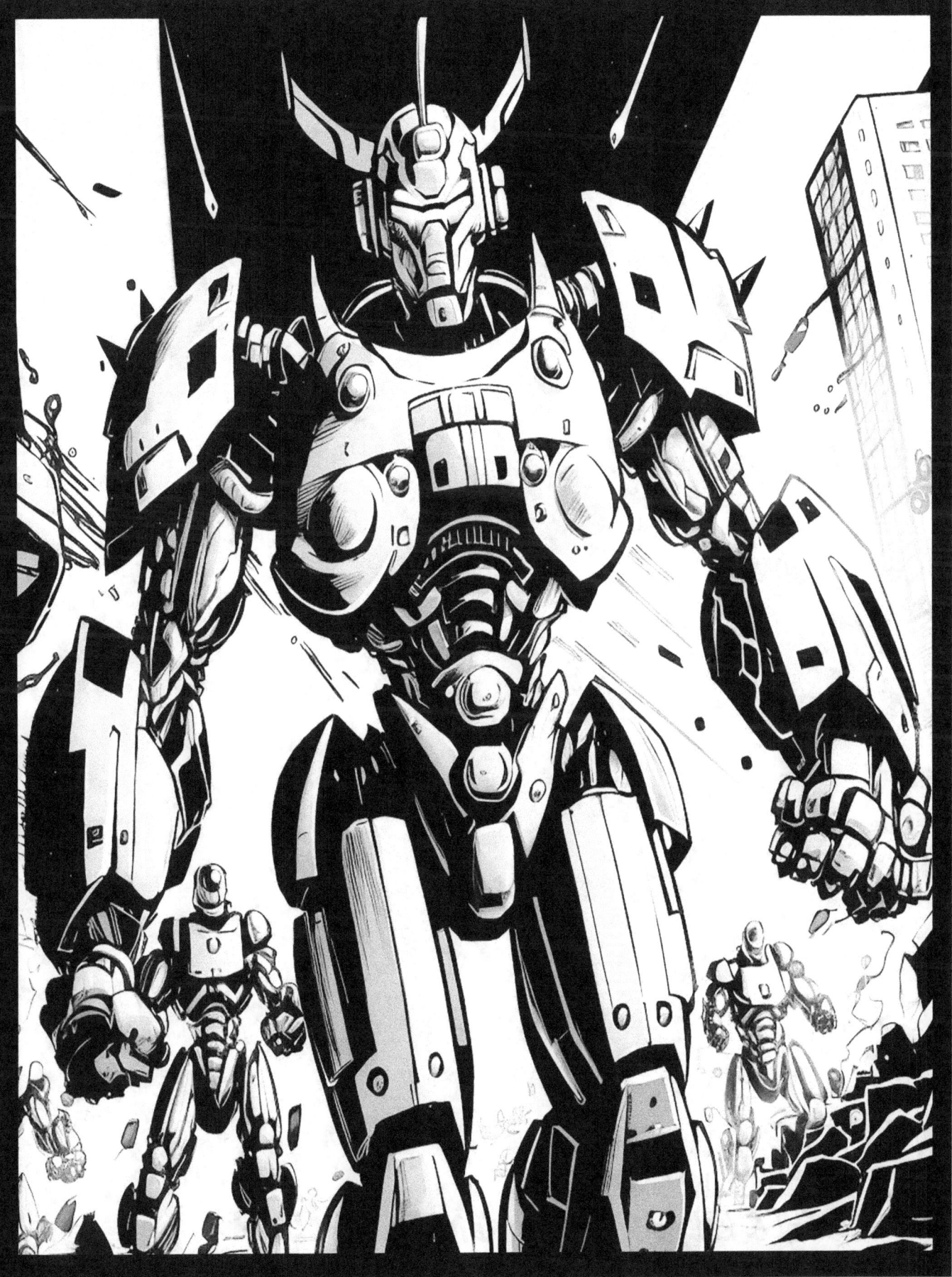

WRONG PLANET
SUBMIT YOUR ART AT:
@IMAGICOLORZ ON INSTAGRAM

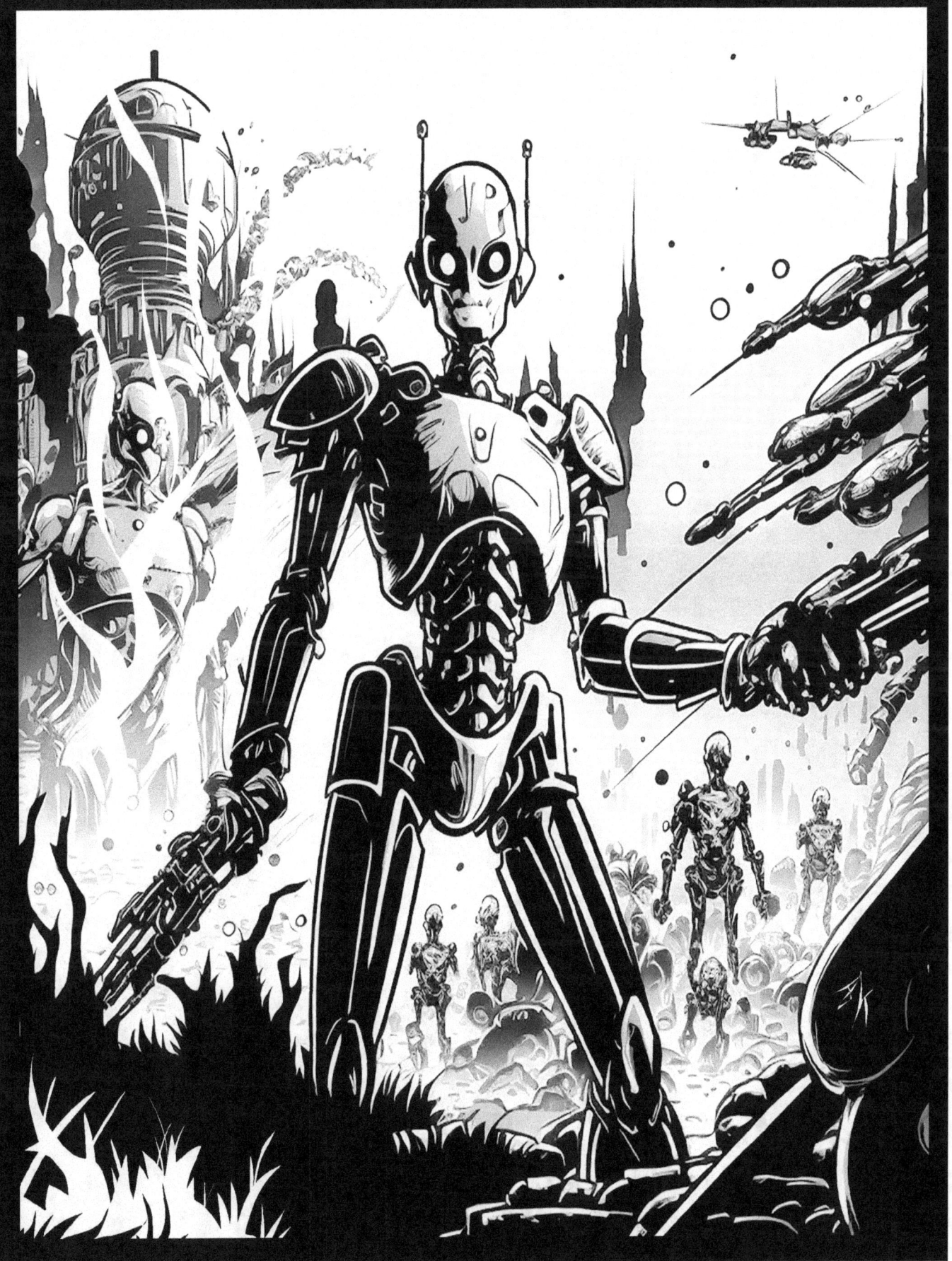

WOLF MECH: WOLF PACK LEGION
SUBMIT YOUR ART AT:
@IMAGICOLORZ ON INSTAGRAM

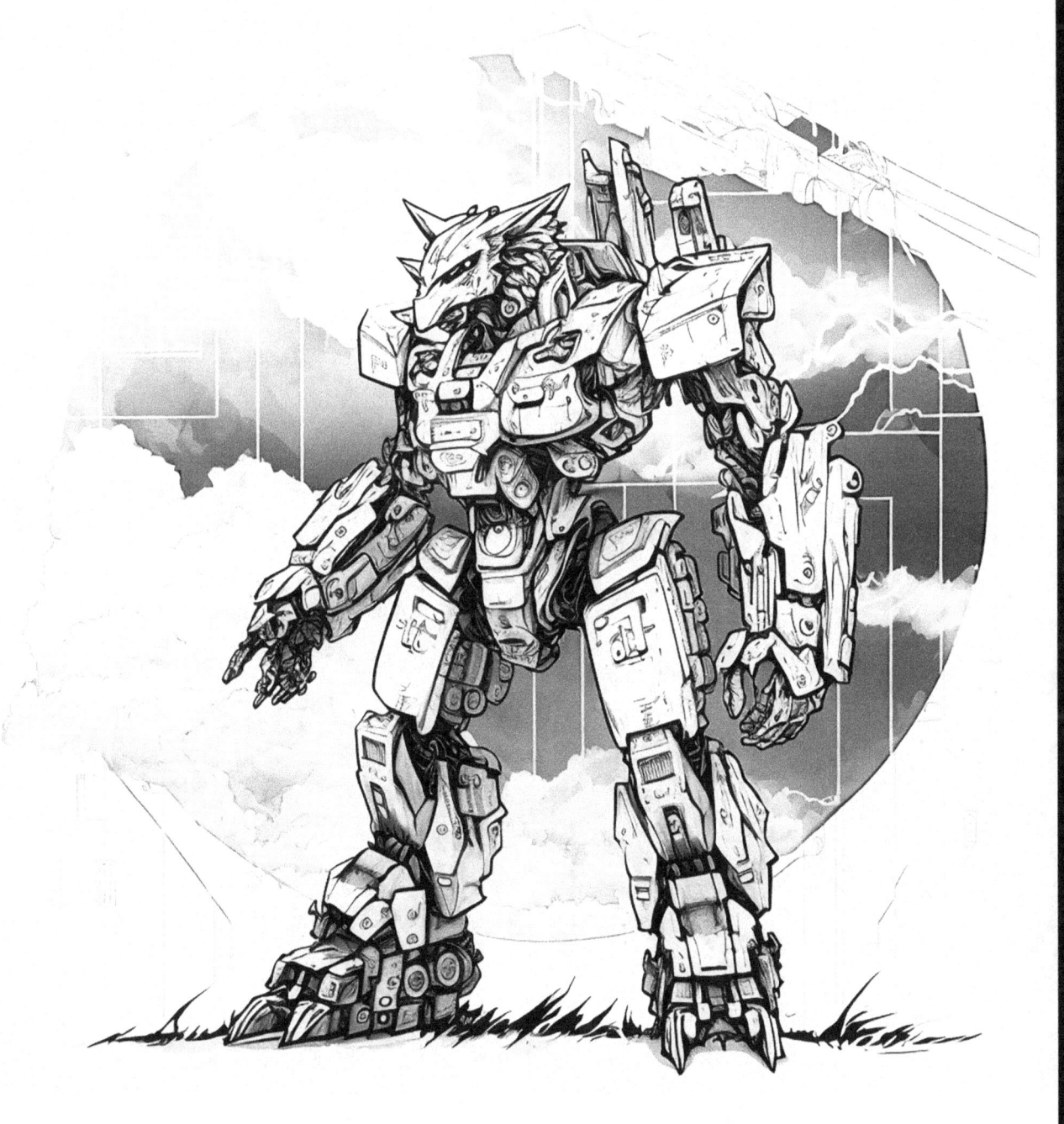

INSIDE THE BIG ONE
SUBMIT YOUR ART AT:
@IMAGICOLORZ ON INSTAGRAM

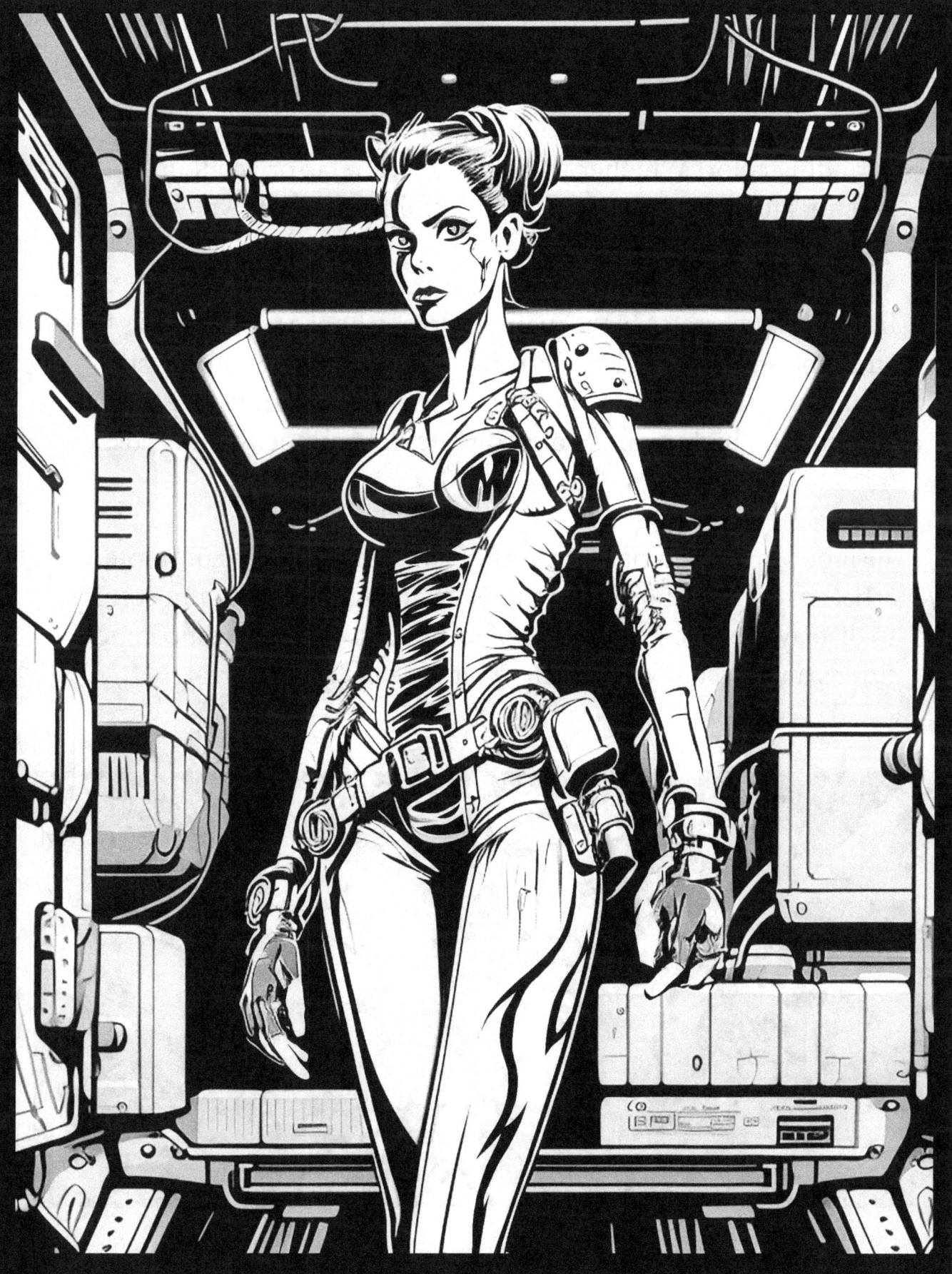

In this coloring book, you will find several highly detailed images of giant robots, alien machines, and battle mechs. The 40 images are begging for you to put your original artistic spin on the page by adding color! Whether you just want to relax or go all in, the potential for precision and detail is unlimited! What will you design?

Imagi-colorz creates high-quality coloring books for hobbyists and professional colorists. Our detailed images promote artistic imagination and a means of expression for all aspiring artists. We recommend high-quality colored pencils, brush pens, and artistic markers for our pages.

Visit our Instagram page @IMAGICOLORZ where we promote artists of all ages and backgrounds by giving them the opportunity to display the colored versions of our pages. We also host competitions and giveaways! We can't wait to see what you create!

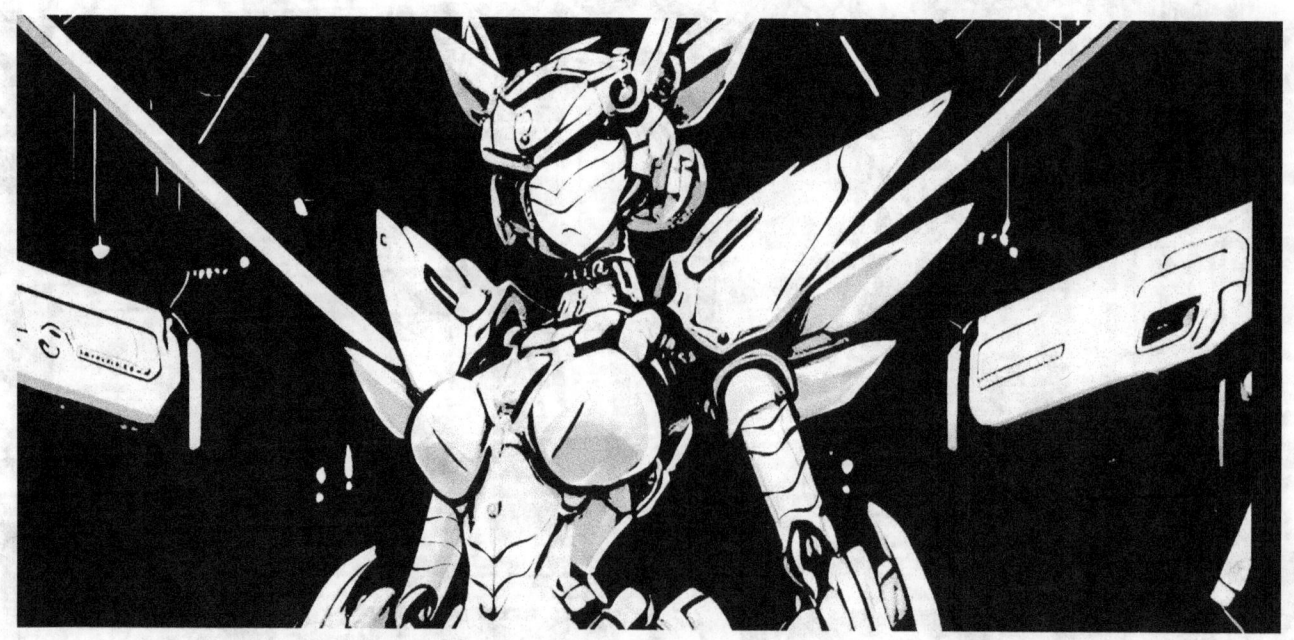